THE JAMESTOWN LECTURES 2006–2007

The Jamestown Lectures
2006–2007

The Rule of Law

The Commercial Bar Association

·HART·
PUBLISHING

OXFORD AND PORTLAND, OREGON
2008

Published in North America (US and Canada) by
Hart Publishing
c/o International Specialized Book Services
920 NE 58th Avenue, Suite 300
Portland, OR 97213-3786
USA
Tel: +1 503 287 3093 or toll-free: (1) 800 944 6190
Fax: +1 503 280 8832
E-mail: orders@isbs.com
Website: www.isbs.com

Hart Publishing, 16C Worcester Place, OX1 2JW
Telephone: +44 (0)1865 517530 Fax: +44 (0)1865 510710
E-mail: mail@hartpub.co.uk
Website: http://www.hartpub.co.uk

British Library Cataloguing in Publication Data
Data Available

ISBN: 978-1-84113-808-4

Typeset by Compuscript Ltd, Shannon
Printed and bound in Great Britain by
TJ International Ltd, Padstow, Cornwall

Foreword

'Jamestown' signifies so many things. The courage of those boarding tiny vessels at Blackwall Stairs on the River Thames, and the vision and ambition of those in the Inns of Court who supported the enterprise. The foundation of 'America' as we know it today. The start of almost inconceivable growth over as short a period as four hundred years. A sheet anchor for the bond that grew between the United Kingdom and the United States of America. The export of the common law and all it stands for.

With the 400th anniversary of the founding of Jamestown, the opportunity arose to pause and reflect on the importance of the rule of law in and to the world. To reflect on the things we have got right because of it and to notice the things we have got wrong where we have lost sight of it. And to celebrate the bond between those involved in the law on each side of the Atlantic.

That bond is in robust good health. A sign is the respect that The Inns of Court in England and Wales and the American Inns of Court have for each other, and their shared purpose in underpinning the practice of law with professionalism, ethics and a sense of responsibility. Another sign is the relationship between the commercial bar of England and Wales and that of North America, as shown by the role that COMBAR and the American Inns of Court have striven to play in marking the occasion of the 400th anniversary.

From April 2006 to April 2007 the 'Jamestown Lectures' organised jointly by COMBAR and the four Inns of Court of England and Wales, shadowed the journey taken from London to Jamestown 400 years ago. Then in April 2007, the University of Richmond and the American Inns of Court welcomed representatives of the United Kingdom's senior judiciary, of the Inns of Court of England & Wales and of COMBAR for a celebration of the arrival of the adventurers, and with it the founding of Jamestown, and in turn of modern America.

COMBAR has marshalled the 'Jamestown Lectures' into this volume. These examine the rule of law in the context of the criminal law (Lord Lloyd of Berwick), the judicial system (Sir David Williams QC) and property and commerce (Mr Keith Clark, of Morgan Stanley and formerly of Clifford Chance). The final lecture, delivered by the Senior Law Lord (Lord Bingham of Cornhill) examines the role of leadership in the rule of law. To the lectures in the series we have added the keynote speech delivered by the Lord Chief Justice (Lord Phillips of Worth Matravers) in Richmond on 11 April 2007, and excellent talks also given in Richmond by two distinguished Judges of the London Commercial Court, Sir Anthony Colman and Sir David Steel, (each a former Chairman of COMBAR) which bring out much of the flavour of the occasion.

COMBAR has produced this volume in order that the insights gained are not lost, in order to add a permanent mark of the anniversary, in order to mark the spirit of collaboration that enabled the lecture series and then the celebrations, and in order to take the opportunity to say 'thank you' from the Commercial Bar of England & Wales to the other organisations involved and to colleagues on both sides of the Atlantic.

There are many who deserve our thanks for the success of the lecture series, and of the celebrations in Jamestown. Of course the lecturers themselves have pride of place in those thanks. We cannot name all others. But we believe all involved will support our decision to mention here Justice Don Lemons of the Supreme Court of Virginia, Justice Randy Holland and Chief Judge Deanell Tacha (respectively the immediate past and the current Presidents of the American Inns of Court), David Carey (Chief Executive of the American Inns of Court), John Hardin Young, the Treasurers, the Under Treasurers and the Benchers of Lincoln's Inn, Inner Temple, Middle Temple and Gray's Inn, David Akridge, Cindy Dennis, Michael Sullivan and Hannah Brown, Christopher Hancock QC (Chairman of COMBAR's North American Committee) and Veronica Kendall (Administrator of COMBAR).

COMBAR would like to dedicate this volume to its Honorary Members from around the world—past, present and future.

William Blair QC	Robin Knowles CBE, QC	Ali Malek QC
Chairman of COMBAR	Chairman of COMBAR	Chairman of COMBAR
2003–2005	2005–2007	2007–

London 21 January 2008

Contents

From left to right: *Robert Seabrook QC, Treasurer, Middle Temple; Roy Amlot QC, Treasurer, Lincoln's Inn; Sir Bernard Rix, former Treasurer, Inner Temple; Lady Rix; Lady Phillips; Lady Justice Arden DBE; Sir Robin Jacob, Treasurer, Gray's Inn; Lord Mance.*
In the distance, just behind Sir Robin Jacob, can be seen a replica of the ship Godspeed (the largest of the three ships to make the voyage to Jamestown from England).
Photo: *University of Richmond School of Law*

Lord Phillips speaking after dinner at the University of Richmond School of Law.
Photo: University of Richmond School of Law

From left to right: *Lord Phillips, Lord Chief Justice of England and Wales; Honourable Sandra Day O'Connor; Honourable John Roberts, Chief Justice of the United States Supreme Court; Lord Mance.*
Photo: University of Richmond School of Law

1

Due Process and the Rights of the Accused

RT HON LORD LLOYD OF BERWICK

Delivered at the Hon Society of the Inner Temple on 8th May 2006

FOUR WEEKS AGO, on Monday 10 April, the US Ambassador unveiled a plaque in the Middle Temple. The Lord Chief Justice, the Master of the Rolls and many other members of the Middle Temple were present, so was the Lord Mayor. The plaque is worth a visit, for it commemorates an event of outstanding importance in the history of England as well as the United States ... the granting of the first charter by King James the First on 10 April 1606 to the Virginia Company of London.

Seven months later the first of the 'adventurers' set forth. There were 144 in all, sponsored, to use a modern term, by the Lord Mayor of the day, and by the 55 livery companies of the City of London. They endured fearful hardships during the crossing. Only about 100 survived the voyage. But it was these few who on 29 April 1607 sailed up the river they named the James, in Cheasapeake Bay, Virginia. On 14 May they founded a settlement they named Jamestown. By the end of 1608 there were only 53 of them left, under the leadership of the redoubtable Captain John Smith. But they had founded the first permanent settlement of English men and women in what is now the United States. There could hardly be a better cause for celebration on both sides of the Atlantic.

I feel honoured and privileged to be giving the first of four lectures that will take place during the next 12 months, one in each of the four Inns of Court. The last will be given by Lord Bingham in Gray's Inn in February 2007. They will all deal in one way or another with the rule of law. The scene will then shift to Virginia, where the final celebrations will take place in May 2007, to mark the 400th anniversary of the landing.

It may be asked why the Inns of Court should be playing a central role in all of this, and why in particular the Middle Temple. The answer is that it was a member of the Middle Temple, Sir Walter Raleigh, who in 1584 named what is now the East Coast of the United States 'Virginia' in honour of Queen Elizabeth. It was another member of the Middle Temple, Sir John Popham, Treasurer of the Middle Temple, and Lord Chief Justice, who played the leading part in the formation of the Virginia Company. A third member of the Middle Temple, Sir Edwyn Sandys, was largely responsible for the drafting of the Virginia Charter. Sir Edwyn did well in life. He built himself a magnificent house at Northbourne Court in Kent, and is buried in Northbourne church. His tomb on the south wall is also well worth a visit. It is among the finest I have seen.

So many of those involved in the early days were members of the Middle Temple that I feel bound to put in a word for the Inner Temple. In a lecture given by Justice Randy J Holland on 28 November 2005, to which I am very much indebted, he claims that the greatest adventurer of them all—Sir Francis Drake—was also a member of the Middle Temple. But in this respect I believe he was mistaken. It is true that Sir Francis was feted by the Middle Temple in July 1586 on his return from America, where he rescued the remnants of Raleigh's unsuccessful colony at Roanoke. But he was already a member of the Inner Temple. He was admitted on 28 January 1582. It seems likely that he was proposed by Sir Christopher Hatton, the man Queen Elizabeth chose for the Lord Chancellor not for any knowledge of the law, but because of the shape of his calf and his skill in dancing. Whether the present Lord Chancellor would qualify under either of those heads, I am not sure. We know that Sir Francis was a friend and protégé of Sir Christopher Hatton because he named the vessel in which he sailed round the world after an emblem in Sir Christopher's coat of arms—the *Golden Hind*.

Since this is the first of four lectures spanning such a momentous year, I hope I may be forgiven for sketching in the historical background. It was, as Dickens would have said, the best of times, it was the worst of times. It was the age of wisdom. It was the age of foolishness. Not for nothing did the King of France call James I the 'wisest fool in Christendom.' Elizabeth, the last Queen of England, had seen off the might of Spain, in what must surely rank as England's finest hour. She had governed England for 45 years through the Privy Council and the prerogative courts and, in particular, the Star Chamber. The Star Chamber did not then have the bad name it afterwards acquired under her successors. Indeed it did much to secure the future of the common law and its judges. And it was the Star Chamber that proclaimed in words that have often been repeated that it were 'better to acquit twenty that are guilty than condemn one innocent.'

Lastly it was Elizabeth who laid the foundations of the Anglican settlement, celebrated and glorified by the poetry of George Herbert, and justified theologically by Richard Hooker—the 'judicious hooker', as he is described on his gravestone, perhaps the most illustrious and certainly the most influential of all Masters of the Temple. By a happy coincidence Hooker and Sandys were great friends. Hooker was his tutor at Oxford, and it was Sandys who paid for the publication of Hooker's great work, *The Laws of Ecclesiastical Polity*.

The reign of James I was something of an anti-climax. It was a time of peace, not war. For the first time English people could seek their fortunes abroad, and did so. It was a time when the Puritans were growing in strength and self-confidence. And they were also becoming increasingly restive under the restrictions imposed by the Anglican hierarchy. If they were going to achieve toleration—as GM Trevelyan put it in one of his essays—they could either go to America or stay at home and make a bid for power. The first of these movements founded the United States. The second founded English parliamentary government.

But there were other forces at work as well. Unlike the settlers in New England the original settlers in Virginia were not, by and large, Puritans or, if they were, their motive was not primarily religious. They were not exiles. Like others after them, they went to American to better themselves, and they remained loyal to the Crown throughout the Civil War and the Commonwealth.

And so I come to 1606 itself. It was the year in which *Macbeth* was first performed at the Globe Theatre in London. It was the year in which Monteverde was putting the finishing touches to his first and greatest opera, *Orfeo*. It was the year in which Caravaggio painted the *Supper at Emmaus*. It was the year in which the plantation of Ulster began in earnest. It was the year in which Guy Fawkes and his colleagues faced trial before the Star Chamber, after enduring horrific torture in the Tower. And it was the year in which King James I granted the London Company of Virginia its first charter.

The charter itself is a fascinating document. It expresses the hope that the settlers may in time bring the infidels and savages living in those parts to human civility and to a settled and quiet government.' Meanwhile the settlers and their children (the reference to children here is important) were to enjoy 'all the liberties franchises and immunities as if they had been abiding and born within this our realm of England.' This was in marked contrast to the colonies established at that time by France and Spain, who were accorded no such liberties. It was these 'liberties' that were re-stated and elaborated in subsequent Charters, and eventually in the Virginia Declaration of Rights of 1776. Since this is a lecture on due process, I cannot do better than read from Article 8:

> That in all capital or criminal prosecution a man has a right to demand the cause and nature of his accusation, to be confronted with his accusers and witnesses … and to a speedy trial by an impartial jury and without whose unanimous consent he cannot be found guilty; nor can he be completed to give evidence against himself; that no man be deprived of his liberty, except by the law of the land or the judgment of his peers.

It will be noticed that the Virginia Declaration of Rights does not refer in terms to 'due process.' But those words are to be found in the constitutions of many other states at that time and are, of course, enshrined in the Fifth and Fourteenth Amendments of the Federal Constitution. I know of no better short definition of what is meant by due process.

What exactly were the 'liberties franchises and immunities' enjoyed by the English people in 1606 that have meant so much in American history? First and foremost there was the Magna Carta of 1215. By chapter 39 King John undertook that he would not proceed against any free man 'except by the lawful judgment of his peers and by the law of the land.' It has been held by the Supreme Court that due process of law in the Fifth Amendment was intended to have the same meaning as the words 'By the law of the land' in Magna Carta. In this the Supreme Court was following good early authority. For a statue of Edward III of 1354 provides that 'no man shall be ... taken or imprisoned ... to put to death without being brought to answer by due process of law.' So due process is an ancient concept in English law; and at the heart of due process lies trial by jury.

Nor was Magna Carta set in stone at Runnymede. The provision of Magna Carta were elaborated in subsequent reigns culminating, so far as England is concerned, in the Petition of Right of 1628 and the Bill of Rights of 1689.

Magna Carta was also the subject of numerous commentaries on both sides of the Atlantic. There were the *Institutes* of Sir Edward Coke in the 17th century and the *Commentaries* of Sir William Blackstone in the 18th. The views of Sir Edward Coke in particular were enormously influential in the United States. He became Chief Justice of the Common Pleas in 1606 and of the King's Bench in 1613.

It was Sir Edward Coke who presided in the great case brought by Dr Thomas Bonham against the College of Physicians in the City of London. The members of the College had the exclusive right to practise medicine in the City of London under an Act of Parliament passed in the time of Henry VIII. Dr Bonham was not a member of the College but he had a degree in medicine—or physic—from the University of Cambridge. When he set up to practise in London he was summoned by the College, and fined 100 shillings. That was in April 1606. In November he was summoned again. This time he was sent to prison where he was kept for seven days. So he brought an action against the College of Physicians of false imprisonment. The defendants relied on their statute, under which they had been given very extensive powers to enforce their rights. But Coke CJ held that the statute was void. He gave a number of reasons, one of which has a familiar ring—that the statute had made the defendants judge in their own cause. Another reason was that no man should be punished twice for the same offence. He encapsulated his views in the following famous sentence:

> And it appears in our books, that in many cases the common law will control Acts of Parliament, and sometimes judge them to be utterly void; for when an Act of Parliament is against common right and reason, or repugnant, or impossible to be performed the common law will control it and adjudge such act to be void.

In support of this view Chief Justice Coke cited numerous earlier authorities in which Acts of Parliament had been held to be void at common law.

The principle laid down by Chief Justice Coke was one by which he set great store. For he came back to it in his *Second Institute*, where he said that any statue passed by Parliament contrary to Magna Carta should be 'holden for none.'

But in England the principle did not survive for long. This is hardly surprising in view of the triumph of Parliament in the civil war. It is true that Dr Bonham's case was cited with approval by Chief Justice Holt, another great Chief Justice, at the beginning of the eighteenth century. But thereafter it disappears from the scene. It could not stand alongside the emerging constitutional principle know as the Supremacy of Parliament.

But if the seed sown in Dr Bonham's case fell on stony ground in England, it fell on good ground in the United States and bought forth fruit a hundred fold. Coke's *Institutes* and the *Commentaries* of Blackstone were widely read by the colonists, most of whom, then as now, appear to have been lawyers. It was Dr Bonham's case that James Otis cited in his celebrated attack on general search warrants in the Superior Court of Boston in February 1761. Although Otis lost the case, there can be no doubt that his speech—a speech that was said to have electrified the continent—made a lasting impression on the young John Adams, who was present in court to hear it. He would surely have had it in mind 20 years later when he was drafting the Massachusetts Declaration of Rights of 1780.

And so one comes to *Marbury v Madison*, decided by the Supreme Court in 1803. It was the turning point in American constitutional history. For it established the all-important principle that it is the Supreme Court that is the final arbiter of the meaning of the Constitution, a point about which there was nothing in the Constitution itself. This enabled Chief Justice Marshall to decide the case on the politically convenient ground that section 13 of the Judiciary Act, a statue passed by Congress in 1789, was unconstitutional and therefore invalid.

Dr Bonham's case was not cited in the judgment. But the Court would have known it well. Looking back one can see now that the principle stated by Chief Justice Coke lay at the parting of the ways. It was the point at which the two constitutions diverged with hugely important consequences for human rights on both sides of the Atlantic. In the United States due process is protected by the 5th and Fourteenth Amendments. If Congress or the states pass legislation that infringes either of these Amendments, the Supreme Court, following *Marbury v Madison*, can say so, and the legislation is 'holden for none.' But in the United Kingdom it is different. Our judges can do their best to construe legislation so as not to infringe due process. But that is all. Even if the legislation (I am referring to primary legislation) is incompatible with the European Convention of Human Rights, the House of Lords can do no more than make a declaration to that effect—a striking manifestation of the Supremacy of Parliament.

But it makes it all the more important that Parliament should ensure that due process is not infringed, that its legislation is compatible with the European Convention, and that suspects as well as those accused of crime should be adequately protected. In the last part of this lecture, therefore, I propose to consider the record of successive governments since the early 1990s, and compare that record with the record of the House of Lords as a judicial body during the same period. I am driven to the conclusion that Parliament does not come well out of the comparison.

I will leave to the end recent legislation against terrorism, a subject in which I have a particular interest. But there is much else that is cause for concern. When I became a judge in 1978 there were 42,000 men and women in prison. There are now nearly 77,000. Many people would regard that figure as a national disgrace. Nobody suggests, I think, that this increase in the prison population is due solely or even mainly to an increase in the crime rate. Nor it is it due to improved detection rates. A more likely cause, I would suggest, are the restless efforts of successive governments to legislate in the field of crime. In the 12 years since 1994 there have been 24 new Acts of Parliament in the criminal field—an average of two a year. Since May 1997 the Home Office alone has been responsible for the creation of 404 new criminal offences. Of course not all these new offences have resulted in prison sentences. But many have.

The creation of new offences is not the only cause for concern. There is also the constant pressure from the legislature for heavier sentences for existing offences. The best example of this is the statutory scheme set out in the Criminal Justice Act 2003 for setting the minimum term of imprisonment to be served by those convicted of murder. This was the Home Secretary's legislative response to the decision of the House of Lords in *R v Anderson*, in which it was held that the Home Secretary should no longer play any part in fixing, and in some cases increasing, the so-called tariff. For him to do so was incompatible with Article 6 of the European Convention on Human Rights.

But I want to give an example from my personal experience. When I first became a judge in 1978 most cases of causing death by dangerous driving were dealt with by a fine. For the more serious cases there might be a short sentence of six to 12 months' imprisonment. The guideline case was called *Guilfoyle*. I know this because the first case I tried at the Old Bailey was just such a case. Nowadays the starting point for the most serious cases would be six or even eight years. It may be said that the responsibility for this increase rests with the judges, not with Parliament. But that would be wrong. For the judges are obliged to have regard to the maximum sentence for any offence, since the maximum sentence fixed by Parliament represents Parliament's view of the appropriate sentence for the worst case of that offence. In 1977 the maximum sentence fixed by Parliament was two years. It was then increased to five years, then 10 years and now 12 years. Since in the short space of a generation the maximum sentence (and this is only one example) has increased six fold, is it surprising that the prisons are full and overflowing? And now we have in addition the new offence of causing death by careless driving, carrying a sentence of five years' imprisonment.

Then there is the recent fashion for fixing minimum sentences. This started in the dying days of the Conservative Government in 1997, with automatic life sentences for those convicted of a serious, violent or sexual offence for the second time, and minimum sentences of seven and three years for repeat Class A drug offenders, and domestic burglars. The Labour Government followed suit in 2003 with a minimum sentence of five years for certain firearm offences. My own view is that Parliament should not be in the business of fixing minimum sentences, because they cannot know the circumstances of the individual case. That was certainly the view of the Chief Justice, Lord Taylor. I would like to quote from his last, unforgettable speech in the House of Lords when he was already gravely ill. 'Quite simply,' he said 'minimum sentences must involve a denial of justice': not, be it noted, the *appearance* of injustice but *actual* injustice. And that was also the view of his successor, Lord Bingham, who expressed his profound anxiety at this new trend.

Another cause for concern is the desire of successive governments to 'improve' (as they say) conviction rates. Take rape. The Government is persuaded that the conviction rate for rape is too low, though how governments can tell how many defendants have been wrongly acquitted I do not know. So what does the Government do? It makes a fundamental change in the substantive law. Under the Sexual Offences Act 2003 it is no longer necessary to prove beyond reasonable doubt that the defendant knew that the woman was not consenting. It is enough to prove that a reasonable person would have believed she was not consenting. So gone is the defence of honest belief. We now have rape by negligence. We have created an offence of utmost seriousness carrying a maximum sentence of life imprisonment, in which the defendant need not have had a guilty mind. Whether conviction rates will in fact be 'improved' remains to be seen. For myself I rather doubt it.

Last in this connection I should touch on procedure. One of the most hallowed rules of our criminal procedure is that a person cannot be compelled to be a witness against himself—the rule against self-incrimination. In the United States it is covered by the Fifth Amendment. In England it is usually referred to as the right to silence. Yet when it was found that terrorist organisations in Northern Ireland were using that right to such an extent that it was becoming difficult to secure convictions, the Conservative Government decided to modify the right to silence. By the Criminal Justice and Public Order Act 1994 it was to be permissible to draw an inference from the defendant's failure to mention a fact that he could reasonably have been expected to mention. The Labour Government has continued

down the same path. It has also abolished the ancient rule against double
jeopardy, another right specifically protected by the Fifth Amendment in
the United States.

In all these respects, whether in the field of procedure, sentencing or substantive law, Parliament has in recent years been tilting the balance more
and more in favour of the victim. In doing so, it has inevitably restricted
the rights of the criminally accused. I cannot think of any other such period
in our recent history. The one shining exception is the incorporation of the
ECHR into our domestic law, for which the Labour Government deserves
full credit.

What is the reason for this ceaseless activity of successive governments in
the field of crime? No doubt they wish to be tough on crime. There could be
no quarrel with that. But they also wish to *appear* tough on crime; not only
on crime in general, but also on particular crimes which happen to have hit
the headlines. Urged on by the media they know that being tough on crime
plays well with the electorate. The problem is that the opposition parties
know this too. The result is a clog on constructive debate. Governments
are always anxious to send out the right 'message.' I sometimes wonder
whether the message ever reaches the criminals for whom it is intended.
I suspect not; and, even when it does, I doubt whether it has much effect.
But it certainly has an effect on the voters.

So far I have said nothing about terrorism. I remember well when
I was writing my report on legislation against terrorism in 1995 I was under
much pressure—especially from members of the Labour opposition—to
recommend that terrorists should be treated as ordinary criminals. Otherwise, it was said, we would make terrorists into martyrs, and thereby serve
their evil purpose. I did not altogether agree with this view. It seemed o me
then—as it does now—that terrorists are a special case, partly due to the
nature of the motivation and partly because their killing is indiscriminate.
So I welcomed the Terrorism Act 2000. It gave the police all the additional
weapons they needed. But it also preserved the essential rights of the suspect. I wish I could say the same for subsequent legislation. We have now
had three new counter-terrorism Acts in five years. So far from treating
terrorists like other criminals, we have now gone much too far in the other
direction.

Take Part Four of the Anti-Terrorism Crime and Security Act 2001. It
was passed in a great hurry in the immediate aftermath of 9/11. It enabled
the Home Secretary to detain suspected terrorists (it did not apply to British
citizens) pending their deportation. But as there was no prospect of them
being deported to their own countries, they were in effect being detained
indefinitely without trial. Such legislation is acceptable in wartime, when
there is a threat to the life of the nation. But we were not at war in 2001.
To talk of the war on terrorism is no more than a figure of speech, like
the war on want. Yes, terrorism is a very serious threat. There can be no

doubt about that; and it is likely to remain so for many years to come. But I refuse to accept that there is a threat to the life of the nation. To deprive a man of his liberty, not because of what he has done but because of what he might do, is a grave step for any government to take in peacetime. The Labour Government could only take that step in 2001 by derogating from the European Convention on Human Rights. We were the only country to do so. In the event the House of Lords held in *A v Home Secretary* that Part Four of the 2001 Act infringed Article 5(1)(F) of the European Convention, and so the derogation order was quashed. It was a critical moment in the relationship between Parliament and the Judiciary. The Home Secretary looked like a man in agony. But he made the right choice. The Government decided to accept the decision. We all breathed again.

But the Belmarsh detainees who had been held for up to four years were not released. They were immediately made subject to control orders. In his first report on the operation of the Terrorism Act 2005 Lord Carlyle has described the obligations which are now imposed in what has become the standard form of control order. 'On any view' he says 'those obligations are extremely restrictive ... they fall not very far short of house arrest, and certainly inhibit normal life considerably.'

Whether such extreme restrictions amount to a deprivation of liberty is a matter for debate. But it may not matter here; for either way one would expect such restrictions to be imposed only as a result of criminal proceedings to the usual standard of proof. But proceedings under the Terrorism Act 2005 are not criminal proceedings. They are civil proceedings. They do not even require the Secretary of State to be satisfied on the balance of probabilities. It is enough that the Secretary of State has reasonable grounds for suspicion. During the debate in the House of Lords I asked whether there was any precedent for imposing what looks like, and must certainly feel like, a criminal sanction as the outcome of civil proceedings. I was told that the nearest precedent was an ASBO.

It is true that the Secretary of State must apply to the High Court for permission to make a control order. But the jurisdiction of the High Court is limited. It can only quash the control order if the Secretary of State's decision was 'flawed' on the material before him, applying the principles of judicial review; and in any event the proceedings in Court are of a most unusual kind. They replicate the procedure before the Special Immigration Appeals Commission. The suspect is not entitled to see all the relevant evidence; he is provided with a 'special representative' appointed by the Attorney-General for that purpose, and the hearing may take place in his absence. In his recent judgment in the High Court Mr Justice Sullivan held that the procedures under the 2005 Act were incompatible with the respondent's right to a fair hearing under Article 6 of the Convention. He described those procedures as providing only a 'thin veneer of legality.' I agree.

I find the control order regime almost as objectionable as Part Four of the 2001 Act, which it replaced. In his recent exchange of emails with Henry Porter in *The Observer*, the Prime Minister excuses, or perhaps I should say justifies, the legislation on the grounds that it has only been applied in a small number of cases. Currently there are only 12 control orders in place. I do not find this justification satisfactory. One might as well say that only 55 people were killed on 7 July.

Like its predecessor, the 2005 Act was rushed through Parliament. The 2001 Act was about to expire, and the Belmarsh detainees would have to be released. The House of Commons did not have time to debate the Bill because it only reached its final form on second reading in the House of Lords. The committee stage in the House of Commons was a farce. The House of Lords did not like the Bill at all. But after an all-night sitting, the House of Lords allowed the Bill to get through on the understanding that it would be brought back early in the next session. But this undertaking was broken. It was overtaken—so it was said—by the events of 7 July. Instead of improving existing legislation, the Government decided to introduce yet more legislation, again in a rush.

And so I come to the Counter Terrorism Act 2006. The two most controversial provisions in the Bill were, first, the so-called glorification offence and, secondly, the power for the police to hold terrorist suspects for up to 90 days without charge. The former goes to the right of free speech under Article 10 of the Convention; the latter goes to the heart of due process under Articles 5 and 6.

I still find it surprising that the Government should have believed that 90 days would be compatible with Article 5 of the Convention. I also find it surprising that they should have accepted so readily the evidence of ACPO that 90 days was what was required by the police. I say that for this reason: as recently as 2003 the police were asked how long they needed in terrorist cases. They answered 14 days. Bearing in mind that the maximum for all other offences, however serious and however complex, is only four days, 14 days seemed to be at the time to be more than enough. But be that as it may, the reasons which the police gave in 2005 for needing 90 days were exactly the same as the reasons which they had given in 2003 for needing 14 days. Yet nothing of relevance had changed in the meantime. When giving evidence to the House of Commons Home Affairs Select Committee neither the Metropolitan Police Commissioner nor ACPO could point to any case where 14 days had not been enough.

I must not leave the subject of terrorism without trying to be more constructive. As I have said there remains a very real threat of further terrorist activity in the United Kingdom. But in my view it is unlikely to be a repeat of the sort of highly sophisticated atrocity which destroyed the Twin Towers on 9/11. The activities of Al Quaeda were disrupted by the invasion of Afghanistan to a much greater extent than is often appreciated.

The threat is, I think, more likely to come from small groups of individuals working alone with homemade explosives, such as occurred in London on 7 July 2005. We must therefore face the fact that such individuals may indeed cause great loss of life, especially if they are prepared to blow themselves up in the process.

Now it goes without saying that it is the first duty of any government to protect its citizens—*salus populi suprema lex*. The questions is how that is best done. It is not, I think, best done by introducing further, ever more repressive legislation. Indeed I think that such legislation will be counterproductive. It will only serve to drive more individuals into the terrorist camp. In the course of many debates on terrorism in the House of Lords, there has been no more remarkable speech than that of Lord Condon, a former Metropolitan Police Commissioner, on an amendment to increase the detention period from 28 days to 90 days. Tactically, he said, it would serve a useful short-term purpose. But strategically it would be a great mistake. It would play into the hands of the propagandists. He said:

> This is not about putting a finite number of people behind bars. This is a philosophical struggle that will endure in my children's lifetime and my grandchildren's lifetime. I do not want us to do anything that will be counter-productive.

So he voted against the amendment. Coming from a former Metropolitan Police Commissioner, this is advice which we would do well to follow.

In his recent exchange of emails with Henry Porter of *The Observer*, the Prime Minister explained the problem as follows: 'we are trying' he said 'to fight twentieth first century crime with nineteenth century means. It hasn't worked—it won't work.' I agree that we should use all the modern methods at our disposal for detecting and convicting criminals. That is why I have long advocated the use of intercept evidence in court. But if by modern methods the Prime Minister means legislation which cuts cross the basic principles on which our criminal justice system is built—the presumption of innocence, the rule against self-incrimination, the right of an accused to hear the evidence against him and so on—then I profoundly disagree. These are not 19th century inventions. They do not change with the changing threat. They are inherent in our perception of justice and the rule of law.

The Prime Minister says he would impose restrictions on those suspected of being involved in organised crime. He would seize the cash of suspected drug dealers and the cars they drive round in, and require them to prove they came by them lawfully. This seems to envisage three classes of citizen—the innocent, the guilty, and suspects. But who decides who is a suspect? The police? And suspected of what? There was evidence in *A v Secretary of State* that upwards of a thousand individuals from the United Kingdom have attended terrorist training camps in Afghanistan in the last five years. Are they all to be treated as suspects?

Then it is said that the civil rights of the suspect must yield to the civil rights of the law-abiding majority. This is a view which was often expressed in the debates in the House of Lords. There is one right that matters more than all the others, it was said, and that is the right to life. But what does this mean? If one could show that by keeping 10 or 100 or 1,000 suspects under house arrest one could save a single life, then the argument would have much force. But it seems to me there is no way of relating one to the other.

So what are we to do? We must remember that even if the 2005 Act had been in force on 7 July 2005 it would not have prevented the London bombing. So what we need above all is better intelligence. We should also make much better use of existing legislation. It works, as we have seen from the trial and conviction of Abu Hamza. The detention of more and more suspects without charge for ever longer periods is not the answer. It will be counter-productive for all the reasons given by Lord Condon. And it will not make us safer.

I turn last to the judges, and in particular the House of Lords in its judicial capacity. We hear so much about the Human Rights Act that we sometimes get the impression that human rights were invented in 1998. We forget that almost all the rights comprised in the notion of due process were first defined and enforced by the judges long ago. Thus if you look in an early edition of *Archbold* you will find a document known to generations of lawyers as the Judges Rules. Long before the Police and Criminal Evidence Act 1984 it was the judges who had laid down the length of time that a suspect could be kept without charge. Thus due process and the rule of law are part of the judicial inheritance; and judges continue to deal with new aspects of due process as they arise. I could give many recent illustrations. I have already mentioned *A v Home Secretary*, the case which more than any other has set the pattern for the future. But there are many other illustrations. I have only time to take three, one from the beginning of the period I am considering, one from the middle and one from the very end.

In *R v Horseferry Road Magistrates Court ex parte Bennett* the defendant was wanted for certain criminal offences committed in England. He was eventually traced to South Africa. The police, after consulting the Crown Prosecution Service, decided not to apply for extradition. Instead they made a deal with the South African police whereby the defendant was arrested and forcibly returned to England by the next airplane. The Divisional Court held that the circumstances in which the defendant had been brought to England were irrelevant. It was not something into which they need enquire. There was some English and a good deal of US authority in favour of that approach.

But the views of the Divisional Court were firmly repudiated by the House of Lords. Lord Griffiths said that if the defendant had been extradited in the normal way there would have been no problem. But the question was whether the judiciary should accept responsibility for the maintenance of the rule of law, and refuse to countenance behaviour that threatened either basic human rights or the rule of law. Lord Griffiths had no doubt that the judiciary should accept that responsibility. He quoted Lord Devlin's observation:

> The courts cannot contemplate for a moment the transference to the executive of the responsibility for seeing that the process of law is not abused.

Accordingly the case was remitted to the Divisional Court to consider whether to impose a stay of proceedings on the ground that the prosecution would be an abuse of the process of the court.

The second case, *R v Looseley* [2001] 1 WLR 2060 concerned entrapment. The question was whether undercover police should be allowed to give evidence of their dealings with drug dealers. Lord Nicholls said:

> Every court has an inherent power and duty to prevent abuse of its process. This is a fundamental principle of the rule of law. By recourse to this principle courts ensure that executive agents of the state do not misuse the coercive, law enforcement functions of the courts, and thereby oppress citizens of the state.

The third case is very recent. I refer to *A v Secretary of State for the Home Department (No 2)*. The question in that case was whether evidence obtained by torture was admissible in proceedings before the Special Immigration Appeal Commission. The Commission held that it was. They relied on rule 44(3) of the SIAC Procedure Rules under which they were entitled to receive evidence that would not be admissible in a court of law. In the Court of Appeal a majority upheld the decision of the Commission.

The decision of the Court of Appeal was reversed unanimously by seven Law Lords in the House of Lords. Lord Bingham said:

> The issue is one of constitutional principle, whether evidence obtained by torturing another human being may lawfully be admitted against a party to proceedings in a British court ... To that question I would give a very clear negative answer.

A little later he said:

> The principles of the common law, standing alone, in my opinion compel the exclusion of third party torture evidence as unreliable, unfair, offensive to the ordinary standards of humanity and decency and incompatible with the principles which should animate a tribunal seeking to administer justice.

He confessed to being 'startled and even a little dismayed' at the suggestion that the deeply-rooted abhorrence of torture at common law could be overridden by a statue and a procedural rule that made no mention of torture at all.

These three cases—there was little or no reliance on the European Convention in any of them: the common law sufficed—show that the courts are a vigilant as they have ever been to prevent an abuse of their process or, putting it the other way round, to secure due process for the defendant in criminal cases. This is what the House of Lords has achieved under the leadership of Lord Bingham and Lord Nicholls. The 'bedding down' of the Human Rights Act was always going to be a critical period for the courts. That too has been achieved. When the history books come to be written, the last decade of the 20th century and the first decade of this will, I think, be seen as a period during which we owed much to the wisdom, strength and humanity of the current members of the House of Lords.

2

Economic Stability and the Creation of Stable Contract and Property Rights

KEITH CLARK

Delivered at the Hon Society of Lincoln's Inn on 7th June 2006

IT IS AN honour and a privilege to be with you here tonight to celebrate the 400th anniversary of the English preparations for the founding of Jamestown. I have been fascinated by the story of Jamestown for a long time. Because basically, of course, it's all about the very early days of globalisation. My own interest dates from the late 1960s. At that time I started working as a trainee lawyer in the City of London. I worked at a firm at the St Paul's end of Cheapside. And in the middle of the day I would walk to Bow Lane for a simple lunch and, on the way, I passed through the churchyard of St Mary Le Bow, which is the main church in the City Ward of Cordwainers right in the middle of the old cockney world. And in the churchyard everyday I met Captain John Smith who stands there in bronze on a plinth with powerful bravado, good strong beard and moustache, long hair, good boots, doublet and cape; and in his hand a book. On the plinth is written:

> Captain John Smith. Citizen and Cordwainer 1580–1631. First among the leaders of the settlement at Jamestown, Virginia from which began the overseas expansion of the English speaking peoples.

I became fascinated by the story: the signing of the Virginia Charter in Middle Temple Hall in 1606; collecting together the intended settlers, many from Kent; the procurement from London financiers and merchants of venture capital, ships and supplies; the voyage across the Atlantic of the three little ships—*Susan Constant*, *Godspeed* and *Discovery*; the arrival of only 105 of the original company of 144 would-be settlers; and then the tough early years graphically described by George Percy (who later became Virginia's governor) in his paper entitled 'Discourse on the plantation of the southern colony in Virginia.' Of course, the great tale from those early years for me, as for many other people, was all about the winter expedition by John Smith when he was captured by Indians and taken to Ponhatan, Chief of the Algonquian-speaking confederacy, who might well have killed Smith. But at the last moment Pocahontas, 'the king's dearest daughter', in the original words of the story 'got his head in her arms, and laid her own upon his to save him from death.'

Anyway, ours is not the job tonight of investigating one of globalisation's first challenges, namely how to reconcile the rights of colonists with the rights of native peoples. Rather, tonight our job is to take note of the mutually shared rootstock between the United States and England symbolised by Jamestown and taking the form of a shared allegiance to the rule of law, a mutual and common law tradition, and a similar approach to governance and to the rights of citizens.

That shared common law tradition has come about over centuries as a result of the endeavours of many distinguished lawyers. This history is well rehearsed by Justice Randy Holland in his speech on Anglo-American Templars Common Law Crusaders, given on Monday, 10 April. Having regard to our distinguished venue tonight I searched the histories to find a particular contribution by Lincoln's Inn in this long process and, of course, I did not have to look further than the first elected president of the settlement, Edward Wingfield, a Lincoln's Inn man. Then, of course, I found William Penn—a member of Lincoln's Inn and, of course, proprietor of Pennsylvania. Penn was strongly influenced by Edward Coke and, in particular, by his reinterpretation of the Magna Carta. And Penn it was who then ensured that the protections of Magna Carta became in 1701 a fundamental part of the Charter of Pennsylvania which, of course, ultimately influenced the constitution of the United States.

Now, the topic I have been asked to talk about tonight against this background is different from Penn's focus: it is economic stability and the creation of stable contract and property rights. And, of course, instinctively we understand this to be a fundamental aspect of the Anglo-American version of the rule of law. But to analyse it we need to distinguish a variety of different strands of enquiry including:

— what legal systems best create stable contract and property rights?
— why do they succeed in doing so?
— what is the relationship between the existence of stable contract and property rights and economic stability?
— and in this regard in particular, is there a necessary conjunction between the creation of stable contracts and property rights and economic stability? Leading on from this, and with reference to the developing world, is the related issue as to whether fostering a legal system that can handle contract and property rights effectively can then deliver economic success.
— if there is a necessary conjunction, then is this conjunction sufficient? Or are there other factors necessary to ensure economic stability over

and above the existence of stable contract and property rights? And, if so, what are they? Indeed can these factors threaten the continuance of economic stability even when stable contract and property rights continue to function?

Well, these are the issues I will attempt to address tonight. And I will do so by addressing them alongside another major theme: the passing of time and the consequences of the continuous deepening of globalisation.

First of all, however, I am mindful that in the current climate of regulatory zeal it is appropriate to disclose interests up front. Accordingly, I should say at this stage of the proceedings that throughout my working career I have practised in the world of financial markets, first of all from the vantage point of a law firm and latterly from the vantage point of an investment bank. It is from this background that I will be addressing this topic tonight. I would also at this stage like to acknowledge my considerable debt in researching this topic to two new books that have recently been published, namely Ross Cranston's book *How Law Works* and Roger McCormick's book *Legal Risk in the Financial Markets* and I have incorporated many ideas and indeed even words from these works in my paper tonight.

I also ought to disclose that I am no economist even if only because as a lawyer I am considerably challenged in the numeracy department.

So this evening I am going to address economic stability via its vital proxy, financial stability, with which I have considerably more familiarity. In doing so I would just point out that financial stability, whilst being a necessary requirement of economic stability, is not sufficient to guarantee it. The Great Depression in the United States proves that. But the financial system does act as a magnifying feedback mechanism on economic stability and indeed instability, as it certainly did during the emerging market crises in the 1980s.

Of course, stable contract rights and stable property rights are fundamental in the world in which I work: the financial markets. Why? Well, banks and financial institutions trade, for the most part, in products that are 'creatures' of the law and in particular contract and property rights. Commercial banks, for example, mainly deal in deposits, debts and similar obligations, of varying degrees of complexity. These rights exist, in law, as 'things' (or 'choses in action') capable of being owned as property only because we, through our financial dealings with each other in the world of contract, bring them into existence. Investment banks largely trade in rights or choses in action constituted under securities and other similar contractual arrangements. When all these rights are enforced, they give rise to debts and claims that may themselves then be owned and traded, and which also owe their existence (and value) to the legal infrastructure that recognises the intellectual concepts that underpin them. They are all the lifeblood of financial business. It is critical for financial business that contract and property rights are stable and certain. To the degree that they are unstable or uncertain they are part of legal risk and a threat to a greater or lesser extent to members of the financial community and their customers. Legal risk now has to be explicitly managed by commercial and investment banks as part of operational risk under the new requirements of Basel II, the new capital adequacy regime being introduced by the banking industry and its regulators. Indeed capital has to be allocated under these new rules to *cover* legal risk. For a bank, therefore, legal risk, when it threatens the legal validity of an 'intangible' asset owned by it or exposes the bank to large claims, is somewhat akin to, say, structural risk for an architect. In the worst case, the bank may lose a great deal of money, its reputation, and the ability to continue in business. And a major loss for a bank, if it threatens a bank's financial survival can challenge the financial well-being of the financial system and ultimately the society associated with it.

However, the nature and impact of such risks is changing over time. We are not dealing with a static world. The financial markets, along with everything else, are subject to enormous and swift developments and changes, arising from the deepening of globalisation.

In the 40 years of my professional life the answers to all the different strands of enquiry that I outlined earlier have been changing quite a lot because the dynamics of investment patterns and business transactions have been changing substantially. The label that is being used to describe the motor for these developments is, of course, the term globalisation. In good practical British style I am not going to philosophise or moralise about this important concept. But I will instance facts. Let me give you a set of snapshots of the City of London over the last 40 years.

When I started in the 1960s. London had its own dominant British commercial bank headquarters, its small sized stockbrokers and jobbers, its small law firms and accountancy partnerships—not to mention the nice long lunch times with flavorsome bottles of wine. And remember that until as recently as 1967 all partnerships were limited in size so that they could not exceed 20 partners. Today's huge UK origin accountancy firms and law firms have developed in 40 years from that miniature platform. Towards the end of Thatcher's Government, Chancellor Nigel Lawson analysed some of the legislative motors engineered by that Government to stimulate deregulation and which drove the growing power of London's financial markets. He said:

> Although financial deregulation is a somewhat imprecise term, it is possible to identify at least ten specific events, of varying degrees of importance that qualify as acts of financial deregulation, most of which occurred during the early part of the government's term of office. In chronological order, these were:

1. The unannounced ending, virtually as soon as the new government took office, of the restrictive guidelines on building society lending.
2. The abolition of exchange controls.
3. The abolition of the so-called 'corset', the supplementary special deposits scheme designed to curb bank lending.
4. The abolition of the reserve assets ratio requirement.
5. The abolition of hire-purchase restrictions.
6. The collapse of the building societies' cartel.
7. Aspects of the Building Societies Act.
8. The ending of the restrictive practices of the Stock Exchange in the so-called 'big bang'.
9. The withdrawal of mortgage lending 'guidance'.
10. The effective abolition of the control of borrowing order.

Two of these events stand out as being of particular importance. The first, most important of all, was the abolition of exchange control. At the time a radical and highly controversial act, it became the norm throughout the major industrial nations of the world—partly because of a genuine belief in freedom and deregulation, partly because the information technology revolution made controls on capital movements increasingly difficult to police. The second was, of course, 'big bang' that gave rise to a huge increase in the sophistication and clout of London's securities markets and (incidentally) to the virtual disappearance of the old British-owned securities houses.

For those of you who would like to read an entertaining overview of this whole period, I recommend Philip Augar's book *The Death of Gentlemanly Capitalism*.

Prior to all of this the City of London, of course, had been at the centre of 400 years of the early form of globalisation, starting with Jamestown. It rested on colonial expansion and the British trading and banking systems. But I would say that it was from the late 1960s that something fundamentally different started to happen. The Euro-dollar markets began to take off in London, largely migrating to London from New York in order to escape the interest equalisation tax that the US fiscal system had imposed on international debt transactions carried out from the United States. American banks and British banks started to create a huge inter-bank market in London denominated in offshore dollars under the tolerant stewardship of the Bank of England that also attracted the larger German, French, Swiss, Japanese and other banks. And when the petro-dollar crises of the 1970s generated vast petro-dollar surpluses in oil-exporting countries, it was this Euro-dollar inter-bank market-based primarily in London that recycled this new wealth in the form of vast loans to balance the books of the oil-importing countries. A global financial rebalancing; followed in the 1980s by a huge global financial restructuring when so many debtor countries defaulted on the 1970s loans.

It was clear at that time that New York and London were the only really powerful international financial hubs in the world, handling between them the bulk of this and other financial effort.

During the 1970s and 1980s also regional Euro-dollar sub-hubs developed for convenience in the Middle East, originally in Bahrain and later in Dubai and in Asia, primarily in Hong Kong but also in Singapore. And in our context tonight it is vital to understand that the lawyers who facilitated the transaction of banking business in these new sub-hubs were exactly the same lawyers who had been servicing this work in London and New York, and that the laws that governed the contracts transacted out of these other hubs were also English law and New York law.

In a recent article Philip Wood pointed out:

> England is only 0.33 per cent of the world's jurisdictions. It occupies less than 0.01 per cent of the planet's land mass and has less than 0.75 per cent of the global population. Nevertheless, if we take the world's most important and biggest international contracts which are syndicated credits, bond issues and to a lesser extent ISDA master agreements—it may be that somewhere between 40 per cent and 70 per cent of international bond issues are governed by English law and the proportion of international syndicated credits may be the same ... English law is the workhorse of international contracts.

I would only add that I think that one of my New York based colleagues like, for example, Lee Bucheit might well with justification say exactly the same thing about New York law.

Now over the last 40 years quite a lot has moved on and looking at the situation today it is clear that there are now three major international financial hubs emerging in the world dealing with a vastly increased flow of financial dealings. They are strategically based in the three different time zones of the United States, Europe and Asia. They are not only New York, London but also Hong Kong. Now, not only are these hubs the central capital-raising engines for their own time zone regions but they compete between each other and interoperate between each other in more and more ways for the smooth working of the world's global financial system that is all interconnected.

Perhaps at this stage this reference to Hong Kong needs a bit more information. If only because the Tokyo Stock Exchange has the second largest market cap in the world, ahead even of London. But this is wholly domestically focussed. Internationally, Hong Kong has become more significant. It is clear that recently the average size of public offerings on the Hong Kong market has overtaken levels in the United States and Europe mainly due to the number of Chinese companies launching multi-billion dollar IPOs. The average amount raised by IPOs in Asia (mainly in Hong Kong but also in Shanghai and Shenzen and Taipei) surged from $83 million in 2004 to $260 million in 2005. This compares with a 22 per cent drop to $170 million in New York last year (both NYSE and Nasdaq) and an 11 per cent rise to $100 million in Europe (mainly London but including continental European markets as well).

These statistics I might add leave out of account last Thursday's launch of the $9.7 billion IPO of Bank of China carried out on the Hong Kong Stock Exchange. The biggest stock offering anywhere of the last six years.

So although tonight, in the spirit of Jamestown, I want to emphasise the importance of the rule of law links between England and the United States, I also want to recognise the new emerging reality that it is the wider common law tradition, including not only London and New York but also Hong Kong, that is underlying the new modern economic stability for the global financial markets.

Why are these major international financial markets centred on the common law geographies of New York, London and Hong Kong?

Well, here we move to the centre of our topic tonight. The financial marketplace can only function properly in an environment that provides a satisfactory level of legal certainty. And it is legal certainty that is best served by the common law, rather than say Napoleonic law or some other system of law. Why? Well, the development of English case law over more than a hundred years has taken place against a background of consistent judicial awareness of a policy objective that, as far as possible, commercial bargains should be enforceable in accordance with their terms and that a successful marketplace does not welcome legal (or for that matter regulatory) 'surprises.' In the course of a judgment that appeared (at least in part) to be intended to address market anxieties about the celebrated dictum of Justice Millett in *Re Charge Card,* Lord Hoffman noted that here 'law is fashioned to suit the practicalities of life.'

Also, mercantile usage or custom has always itself been an important source for English commercial law. An example of the practicality and flexibility and predictability that results from this, which is of enormous importance to bankers, can be found in the law relating to negotiable instruments, which expressly recognises that the categories of negotiable instruments are not closed and new instruments can be added to the list which, in a sense, updates itself in line with the custom and practice of the market. Examples of instruments that are negotiable as a result of mercantile usage include treasury bills, bearer bonds, share warrants, and negotiable certificates of deposit. The common law follows, and automatically adjusts to, market practice. The virtues of English and also New York and Hong Kong commercial law are seen to give London and New York and Hong Kong a significant 'edge' because of the 'certainty' qualities of the common law system. In a letter, dated 1 September 2003, addressed to Lord Woolmer (the Chairman of a House of Lords subcommittee concerned, amongst other things, with the European Commission's 'Financial Services

Action Plan'), Lord Browne-Wilkinson (the chairman of the Financial Markets Law Committee, and, prior to his retirement, the UK's senior law lord) observed that,

> wholesale financial markets require, and by their regulators are required to exhibit, an unusually high level of 'to-the-minute' and 'to-the-penny' legal certainty. English commercial law offers its users the opportunity to achieve a level of legal certainty greater than in almost any other walk of life.

Comparable sentiments are frequently echoed in the language used by the judges themselves in their judgments. For example, in the case of *Scandinavian Trading Tanker Co AB v Flota Petrola Ecuatoriana*, Lord Justice Goff noted:

> It is of the utmost importance in commercial transactions that, if any particular event occurs, which may affect the parties' respective rights under a commercial contract, they should know where they stand. The court should so far as possible desist from placing obstacles in the way of either party in ascertaining his legal position, if necessary with the aid of advice from a qualified lawyer, because it may be commercially desirable for action to be taken without delay, action which may be irrevocable and which may have far-reaching consequences. It is for this reason of course that the English courts have time and again asserted the need for certainty in commercial transactions—for the simple reason that the parties to such transactions are entitled to know where they stand, and to *act* accordingly.

Of course, this important aim of legal certainty is assisted by many different facets of the operating common law system including:

— the notion of freedom of contract;
— the operating practice of specificity of contractual drafting upheld by the courts;
— the technical construction of contracts leading to the limited recharacterisation of business deals;
— and finally, but by no means least, good judges, lack of corruption, and good court systems.

It is against this background that there has come into existence under the common law systems of London, New York and Hong Kong a vast virtual world of rights and duties and operations living in the form of a huge multiplicity of privately created agreements. The modern financial markets rest upon billions upon billions of intermeshing privately created agreements. For example, the contracts between creditors and debtors take many different forms, varying from relatively simple loan agreements and floating rate notes through to complicated swaps, forwards and other derivative transactions. Property rights relating to the equity and other rights in companies are created by contracts setting up the constitution of the companies.

The operations of the exchanges where dealings in these contractual and property rights frequently take place are framed by complex contractual arrangements. Many areas of complex financial business incorporate standard form codes like ISDA that again take effect as contracts.

The ingredients of this vast virtual world of the modern financial markets of rights and duties and operations has been created by private lawyers, many of them working in the large US and UK origin law firms that service the financial markets. They share a common language. They share a common method of drafting. They share the same conceptual legal world. They share similar judges and similar court systems. And they produce comprehensive specifically-drafted financial contracts that synthesise and correspond with astonishing accuracy. It is this vast virtual world of interoperating detailed, precise and yet all-embracing agreements that is the result of the shared traditions of common law lawyers from New York and London.

This is now the virtual world of the financial markets everywhere, not only New York and London. It has been exported. It has been the basis of the operations of the new regional hubs I mentioned earlier. Now it is also the basis of operation of the financial markets in other major centres like Tokyo and Frankfurt. Sometimes the contracts are expressed to be governed here by local law. But the contents derive from common law precedent. And, more frequently, they are expressed to be governed by New York or English law. Whichever law is expressed to govern them, the contracts are almost invariably similar with the same boilerplate protections against a myriad of risk factors. The contents have been essentially driven by the experiences and practices of London and New York.

This creation of this new vast virtual world in the financial markets has occurred in the course of the last 40 years, one-tenth of the time since the founding of Jamestown, but based on the same rootstock of the Anglo-American social and legal model symbolised by Jamestown. Because we are here tonight in Lincoln's Inn I would like to clarify that my references to this legal model include references to equity as well. And it would be wrong not to pay tribute to the enormous versatility and usefulness of the law of trusts as applied to the financial world.

Why is it that New York and London common law has created this virtual financial world and not Napoleonic or some other system of law?

Obviously a lot has to do with geo-political and business reasons. But I also think that from the legal point of view it has been significant that these other systems of law do not share the characteristics of certainty I talked about earlier. They rely upon methods that are guided by the interpretation of very generally expressed provisions of legal codes. Those legal codes are usually capable of different interpretations and different applications to similar fact situations. Also the civil law system does not operate the same strict rules of precedent that operate in England or the United States. So there is a less clear legal framework. Also contracts in the civil system are frequently expressed in a general and not particularly detailed way that means that the myriad of risks expressly catered for in common law contracts are often not expressly addressed in civil law contracts and civil law courts are often presided over by career judges who usually have little experience of the financial world. It is the resulting imprecisions that have caused the financial markets to seek to base themselves upon the comparatively greater certainties created by the common law tradition.

But, as I said, the virtual financial world created by the common law traditions now operates globally irrespective of country, jurisdiction, nationality, surrounding politics or legal system.

Which has many implications, implications that are so recent and so complex as to defy immediate cognition. But, of course, one implication is that business can migrate between financial markets quite easily. In the 1960s and 1970s the only place that the international debt markets could move to from New York when the US authorities imposed the interest equalisation tax was London because of the shared business, culture and legal system. Now it could move to many different locations.

So there is a need for constant vigilance to reinforce the regimes of legal certainty in London and New York.

The requirement to maintain certainty and lack of ambiguity in the operation of the financial markets is so important that it cannot be left to the usual operation of the legal system. Because, however good the laws are and however good the judges are, occasionally the law will get itself into a muddle, which happened particularly in the London markets as a result of the unfortunate decision of the House of Lords in the *Hammersmith v Fulham* case.

This was a House of Lords decision on an ultra vires point—specifically, the power of the local council in question to enter into 'swap' transactions. The case arose because this power was challenged by the auditor appointed by the Audit Commission. Lord Goff has provided a succinct summary of the nature of an interest rate swap:

> Under such a transaction, one party (the fixed rate payer) agrees to pay the other over a certain period interest at a fixed rate on a notional capital sum; and the other party (the floating rate payer) agrees to pay to the former over the same period interest on the same notional sum at a market rate determined in accordance with a certain formula. Interest rate swaps can fulfill many purposes, ranging from pure speculation to more useful purposes such as the hedging of liabilities.

The judgment of the House of Lords in the *Hammersmith v Fulham* case determined that a local authority had no power whatsoever to enter into a swap transaction, or a related transaction, in any circumstances whatsoever. The House concluded that the entry into swap or similar transactions could not be said to 'facilitate' or be 'conducive' or 'incidental' to the discharge of any local authority function.

The case led to unexpected losses that at least in some instances were a complete surprise and were viewed with outrage by banks involved. Local authorities were, after all, seen as a form of UK sovereign credit by many of them. How could it be that another arm of 'government' (the judiciary) would allow them to walk away from obligations freely and openly entered into on the (perceived) pretext of a technicality? Within a few months of the decision (in April 1991), the Bank of England (which was reported to be advocating retrospective validation of the swap contracts by legislation in order to 'preserve the good name of the London markets') reacted to the *Hammersmith v Fulham* case by arranging for the formation of the Legal Risk Review Committee (LRRC) whose terms of reference included:

— reviewing existing law in the light of current practice (domestic and international) in the financial markets and identifying areas of obscurity and uncertainty;
— examining the options in relation to such areas and proposing solutions; considering means by which legal certainty can be speedily and effectively established; and
— considering means by which changes and developments in financial markets practice and future legislation can be reviewed regularly to identify prospective problems and propose appropriate remedies in good time.

The Legal Risk Review Committee has morphed into the Financial Markets Law Committee. It still operates under the auspices of the Bank of England and in all its personifications it has carried out admirable work. The current Chairman is Lord Woolf, ex Lord Chief Justice, and Lord Browne-Wilkinson was his predecessor and members include leading barristers, partners in City law firms, general counsel in financial institutions and representatives of trade associations and governmental departments.

I will briefly refer to two recent examples of its work. It was in the aftermath of 9/11 that governments considered the robustness of the operation of their financial markets and the Treasury here in the United Kingdom issued a green paper requesting comments on a proposal that in the aftermath of a major market disruption, the UK government should be empowered to suspend the performance of contracts in the financial markets and to suspend the operation of financial exchanges—a huge, daunting proposition. Prima facie, one can see that this could be viewed as potentially helpful as an increase in the armoury of measures that could be deployed in an emergency. However, the financial industry became extremely alarmed at the potential uncertainty that could ensue from any invoking of such a process, and a task force was set up under the chairmanship of Sir Andrew Large, then Deputy Governor of the Bank of England. The ensuing work of the working parties of this task force was enormously benefitted by the Financial Markets Law Committee that galvanised considerable resources in the City of London to assist in the detailed evaluation of the contracts operating in the City, the workings of the exchanges and the technical aspects of the legislative framework. As a result of all this work it was decided not to go forward with the original proposals but to rely upon the continued functioning of the markets. It was considered that the contracts governing the markets and transactions had already allocated the risk of major disruption and the risk should be allowed to fall as so allocated.

A very recent case concerns a European proposal, the new Rome Convention, to create a new regime for conflicts of law in Europe. A draft provision (Article 8(3)) in the proposed convention would, if subscribed to by the United Kingdom, replace the current certainties concerning the choice of English law as the governing law for so many of the world's financial transactions by vesting in judges a discretion as to whether to apply this chosen law or instead to apply some mandatory rule of some country closely connected with the relevant transaction—in other words a recipe for muddle. Down to the good work of the FMLC, the UK government has been alerted to the dangers and it has decided not to bind itself by the terms of this proposal.

It is interesting to note that there is a sister committee of the FMLC operating in New York, and recently the European Commission in Brussels has started to investigate whether it would be a good idea to set up a similar group to assist with the operation of the new European securities legal framework.

So certainty is buttressed under the Anglo-American legal model not only by the functioning of the legal system itself but by these further protective devices.

So at this stage we can start to see clearly that the ability under law to create stable contracts and property rights is a necessary requirement for the creation of financial and therefore economic stability. I would now like to move on and explore the issue as to whether the common law success story can be exported to or emulated by other countries, particularly developing countries. Can economic development and stability be created by transforming legal systems to enable them to sustain stable contract and property rights? And I am particularly indebted here to Ross Cranston's analysis.

Well, extrapolating from the successes of the Anglo-American rule of law model in recent decades, a conventional wisdom has evolved, linking for developing countries the rule of law with economic growth, sustainable development and poverty alleviation.

Multilateral financial institutions like the World Bank, regional development banks and some non-governmental organisations have been advocating for emerging and developing countries good governance, one aspect of which is a legal system of a type associated with states operating under the rule of law. This entails a legal system with an independent, impartial, and non-corrupt judiciary, laws that are clear, publicly available and in accordance with the constitution and human rights, and a court system that is accessible and efficient, protects contractual, property and human rights and provides for judicial review of government action. Some people, like Professor Amartya Sen, would contend that rule of law reform along these lines must be valued in itself as part of the process of development, not just for the way it may aid economic or any other types of development. Another line of argument from sources like the Asian Development Bank is that rule of law reforms, by themselves, are only part of the story. What is also needed is legal empowerment of the disadvantaged, which will benefit them in a broad array of development fields that may not have a strict legal dimension such as education, public health promotion, and agriculture.

And there is, of course, historical evidence of a link between law and economic development, for example Singapore and Hong Kong. Yet the relationship between rule of law reform and economic development is complex. It may be that in some respects it is economic development that facilitates a better functioning legal system, or that factors such as investment or political change move both economic development and legal reform in the same direction. Another difficulty with causation in the thesis is identifying the relevant factors in the relationship. Is the key to economic growth the symbolic value of new law on the books, or is the effectiveness of legal institutions in practice more significant? Is governmental accountability, not least through the courts, a necessary element of the rule of law and, if so, how do we explain the East Asian model of economic development, best exemplified these days by China. Further there is a puzzle of foreign investors, who are important in bridging the gap between investment and savings. While they say that they want a legal system that has a clear framework for contracting, which protects contract and property rights, and which provides for the timely resolution of disputes, in practice the existence of business opportunities means that they may invest heavily in countries where these basic features of the rule of law are absent. But, let's face it, this has historically not led to continuous economic stability. Let's remember the 1980s.

In theory law should have an impact on development by facilitating economic activity through encouraging savings and assisting in the allocation of capital. Yet as Ross Cranston says, law's contribution to development in practice is a long-term and tortuous process. As a matter of public policy it demands a sensitivity to its inherent limits, the context in which it operates and the force of other social and economic factors and protecting contractual and property rights may simply shield what a powerful, and possibly corrupt, elite has seized under the cover of state power.

All of this militates against a notion that economic development follows from a blind transplant of western legal models to developing and emerging economies. It cannot be assumed that their introduction will automatically occasion sophisticated economic transactions, foster the establishment of complex enterprises or further the resolution of legal disputes. This is quite apart from the adverse reaction that could follow because transplanting western law might be interpreted as a form of neo-colonial domination.

It is clear, however, that transplanted law will have a greater chance in the commercial area, in particular the investment and financial sectors. But even here commercial laws that impact on rights in the wider community are likely to be resisted. Security and insolvency laws fall into this category, particularly, for example, if they threaten employees' continued employment in a jurisdiction that has no social security system.

Now I would like to turn to the issue of whether a legal system that operates stable contracts and property rights is sufficient in itself to guarantee economic stability and permanence in the operations of vital international financial markets? We have seen that it is necessary. But is it sufficient? At this stage I would like to suggest that not only are stable contract and property rights not in the present stage of the markets' development sufficient to guarantee economic stability but that furthermore if the protection of the stability of contract and property rights focusses too narrowly on the effects generated solely in a national economy or jurisdiction it will miss the bigger picture, namely the emergence of functioning and competing global markets and the economic stability that now has to be measured by reference to this new global reality—essentially because the old days when individual countries had individual legal systems and individual court systems and individual securities exchanges and individual home state-owned companies and service sectors are gone. Globalisation has done for them.

I would like to examine the recent story of the international equity market. It was until recently predominantly located in New York. In telling this story I am going to lean heavily on the testimony of Marshall N Carter, Chairman of the Board of the New York Stock Exchange. Mr Carter gave his testimony, to the Financial Services Sub-Committee on Capital Markets, Insurance and Government sponsored enterprises of the US House of Representatives in Washington in April of this year.

He asserts that from every vantage point evidence of loss of US competitiveness in the capital formation process in the increasingly global marketplace is real and growing. In 2000, nearly half, 46.8 per cent, of global IPO equity was raised on US exchanges. However, in 2005 only 5.7 per cent of the dollars raised by non-US company IPOs was raised through shares listed on US stock markets subject to US regulatory rules and oversights. In addition, of the top 24 global IPOs in 2005:

— only one was registered in the US;
— all of the top 10 were outside the US public markets;
— eight of the top 10 raised capital in the United States via private placements and therefore were not accessible to the average investor foreign companies seeking to delist from the US exchange;
— the number of companies with American depositary receipts on US exchanges has declined 8.8 per cent since 2002.

I would personally add at this stage that this trend continues as shown by the launch of the Hong Kong Stock Exchange last Thursday of the $9.7 billion IPO of Bank of China, which I have already mentioned.

Marshall N Carter identified four explanations for this dramatic situation:

The first is persistent concerns surrounding the US trial bar and the litigious environment in the United States. The total value of settlements in securities litigation and class action law suits has, for example, continued to increase from $150 million in 1997 to $9.6 billion in 2005.

The second reason is the lack of convergence in international accounting standards. This divergence becomes all the more important according to Mr Carter in this period when European countries are moving towards a common standard. When companies today are required to reconcile their accounts with US GAAP when they list in the United States, many baulk at what they consider needless and costly redundancies in reporting.

The third explanation is the improving quality and depth of non-US equity markets. European markets in particular are being helped by the success of the new single European currency. Also Europe has developed robust home-grown sources of capital. The London Stock Exchange's small-cap growth market, known as AIM, saw a tripling of the number of overseas listings in the past two years with more than 220 foreign companies listing.

Fourthly, foreign companies are unquestionably concerned about the costs and added regulatory burdens associated with the US regulation, including, but not limited to, Sarbanes-Oxley. US regulatory costs are especially high in practice because of the overlapping of multiple regulatory enforcement bodies to which public companies are subject, especially post-Enron. The consequence of all this is that the international equity business has moved mainly to London but also to Hong Kong. This, of course, helps to explain why the New York Stock Exchange and Nasdaq are so keen to amalgamate with European exchanges.

I would like to add a few more comments about this fourth point.

We are getting used in the United Kingdom to having a single regulator for all of the financial services. The Financial Services Authority, now in its fifth year, has been showing the benefits in terms of coherence and efficiency of having a single regulator for banking securities and insurance—also a regulator that understands the importance of prudential supervision as well as enforcement.

In the United States you have multiple regulators in this space: the Fed, the SEC, the Thrift supervisor, the Justice Department, the separate attorneys-general of each state. And each state also has its own separate insurance regulator. This structural complexity has been allied over the last five years with heightened regulatory zeal.

Also Sarbanes-Oxley was introduced post-Enron and Worldcom in order to ratchet up various aspects of corporate governance. It does many sensible things like creating an oversight board for the auditing industry and increasing the importance of independent directors on boards of companies. But some of the measures have proven very costly in practice—in particular, Section 404 requiring certification and auditing of due processes and control.

When the London Stock Exchange surveyed 80 international companies that conducted IPOs in London recently it reported that 90 per cent preferring London over New York felt that the demands of US corporate governance rules made listing in London more attractive.

So we see from this story that a financial market as sophisticated and powerful as New York cannot ignore global competitiveness. The legal certainties of the common law tradition can be trumped by uncertainties and cost burdens imposed by legislative and regulatory authorities. Now that Hank Paulson, Chief of Goldman Sachs, is being installed as US Treasury Secretary we will have to see whether the tide will shortly turn in the United States.

Now here in Europe we are dealing with different challenges.

Let me move on to discuss the implications for our topic of the creation of the European single securities market. This increased co-ordination on a regional basis in Europe is, of course, one of the many modern faces of globalisation. And the European agenda is driven not only by business incentives. There is also, of course, a dynamic political impetus.

So far as concerns the financial markets, the last seven years have witnessed an extraordinary process of European integration. The Financial Services Action Plan was launched in 1999, comprising 43 major rule-making measures with the goal of completing the single market in wholesale financial services by end 2005. That target was met in terms of the passage of the high level European legislative measures. Now the practical implementation through member states is taking place. And the target date for implementation of the central directive—MiFID—is November 2007.

These 43 measures cover: market structure, prudential standards and conduct of business requirements.

Although there are imperfections in the measures and although some of the plan awaits detailed implementation it is nevertheless clear that the plan is proving to be a success and should secure benefits originally envisaged in terms of increased efficiencies and opportunities created by such a large financial market operating on common standards.

Now, clearly, a large-scale market change like the Financial Services Action Plan has potential impact on the stability of contract rights and property rights. Indeed quite a lot of the time of FMLC is taken up with seeking to identify and then deal with potential lack of clarity or ambiguity arising from the Financial Services Action Plan.

The laws of the EU must now be taken into account to a large extent in relation to the operation of London's financial market. EU directives are now the single largest source of regulatory change in the market. And the process of harmonisation gives rise to legal risk in its own right. As Lord Browne-Wilkinson has noted, community legislation sometimes seems to fall short of the certainty standards required in the financial markets because of 'the purposive, teleological approach to the interpretation that applies to community legislation.' The continental European legal tradition, rooted in civil law concepts, is very different to the English common law in many important respects. And the implementation across the community of a concept that is intended to have the same effect in each country is, technically, a very difficult exercise when the subject-matter includes the many intellectual constructs involved in financial transactions. But the development of the single financial market in the EU is, as I have said, a political imperative and law is in fact the main tool being used for the purpose of achieving the objective. And English legal developments in important areas such as set-off and netting have, as time has gone by, gradually started to influence, and be influenced by, legal policy in the EU as a whole. Also, as I have explained earlier, the vast virtual world of the interlocking agreements that constitute the business of the European financial markets continues to be shaped by the English and common law competencies.

The maintenance and development of sound financial law in the United Kingdom has to be undertaken in tandem with the maintenance and development of sound financial law for the EU as a whole. But we in England need to be vigilant and to discipline any undue encroachment of European law on the effective continued operation of the common law in our financial markets.

I have already referred to the work of the Financial Markets Law Committee in resisting the dangers of the proposed new Rome Convention.

I would also venture to claim that the whole concept of trying to create a new pan-European contract law that has had its advocates is a step too far. It is too risky, certainly so far as concerns the financial markets. It cannot but create legal uncertainty. And it is unnecessary. The European financial markets already have a perfectly good work horse for their contractual arrangements. That work horse governs the already existing virtual world of the European financial markets. It is called English law.

Now I would like to move to my conclusion. I would like to take the major theme of the passing of time and now project time forward.

What do we see in 40 years time—another tenth of the time between Jamestown and ourselves—so far as concerns economic stability and stable contract and property rights?

I think we probably see fully globalised market economies; driven predominantly by the major markets of the US, Europe and China, not to mention Brazil, Russia, India and Japan. And I think we see dominant financial hubs operating in the three key time zones in the Americas, Europe and Asia. And furthermore the markets have become much more efficient and cost effective. A company, wherever headquartered, can raise capital at the same time from the capital markets in the Americas, Europe and Asia using the same financial statements, the same prospectus and the same procedures. The financial intermediaries will be subject to substantially similar disciplines and requirements in the Americas, Europe and Asia. And an investor, wherever headquartered, will be able to invest directly via each of these hubs and assume for profit risks which arc systematised on a unitary basis throughout the globalised financial markets.

In other words contract rights and property rights will have become stabilised across the global capital markets. And a greater degree of economic stability will be a feature of those globalised capital markets—although we have to believe that there will continue to be cycles of boom and bust.

And I would venture to say that we are already some way down the road to that impending state of affairs (although regulatory convergence will take quite a while) and the critical breakthrough will only come with mutual recognition of accounting standards.

New York will soon reassert the power of its role. London will fulfill the position as Europe's leading financial centre. And Hong Kong will continue its journey of becoming Asia's major financial centre. And the legal foundation will continue to be the essential common law competencies and the Anglo-American approach to the rule of law.

That is why it is right tonight in this context, certainly so far as concerns the financial markets, to celebrate the founding of Jamestown 400 years ago. It symbolises the creation of the common rootstock between England and the United States, our shared rule of law—common law tradition. It is the legal motor that has historically driven the operation of the world's leading financial markets and is now facilitating the full globalisation of those financial markets. Accordingly, it is a major engine also for our shared financial and economic stability.

And in my view in the light of the facts outlined tonight it is going to continue to perform these vital functions for the foreseeable future.

3

The Rule of Law: Independent and Stable Judicial Systems

PROFESSOR SIR DAVID WILLIAMS QC, DL

Delivered at the Hon Society of Gray's Inn on 18th October 2006

INTRODUCTION

THREE HUNDRED AND fifty years after the first permanent English settlement in the United States, I visited Jamestown on Tuesday, 20 August 1957 as the culmination of a day's tour which also included Yorktown and Williamsburg. Today I am privileged to be playing a small part in the 400th Anniversary celebrations which will, of course, reach their climax in 2007. In particular, I wish to express my gratitude to the Jamestown 2007 British Committee and to Gray's Inn for giving me the opportunity of participating in these historic celebrations.

At the outset it is worth noting that Jamestown is in Virginia, a state that has contributed so much to the ambitions, the culture and the constitutional leadership of the United States. Two hundred years after the settlement, for instance, the President of the United States—he had been born in Shadwell, Virginia—was Thomas Jefferson, who in his lifetime was the author of the Declaration of Independence and the self-styled father of the University of Virginia at Charlottesville. Also in 1807 the Chief Justice of the Supreme Court—who had been born in Germantown, Virginia—was John Marshall. He served in that role from 1801 to 1835 and, to the displeasure of President Jefferson, he laid the foundations of constitutional judicial review in his opinion in *Marbury v Madison* (1803)[1] and strengthened the role of the Supreme Court in the course of his lengthy tenure.[2]

The genesis of constitutional judicial review can be argued about at length, but it is clear that the constitutional movements of the 17th century in England undoubtedly influenced politicians and lawyers on the other side of the Atlantic. The seeds of many ideas which reached maturity in

---

[1] I Cranch 137 (1803).
[2] See, on the differing views of Jefferson and Marshall, Arthur E Sutherland, *Constitutionalism in America. Origin and Evolution of its Fundamental Ideas* (1965) 318–41; Albert J Beveridge, *The Life of John Marshall* (1919) Vol 3, esp ch 3 ('Marbury Versus Marshall'); Robert Lowry Clinton, *Marbury v Madison and Judicial Review* (1989).

American constitutional law were sown in what could be called the Anglo-American century, not least with regard to the notion of constitutional judicial review and in the emergence of modern perspectives on the rule of law. At the time of the Jamestown settlement the Chief Justice of the Common Pleas in England, appointed in 1606, was Sir Edward Coke who is nowadays celebrated as an imaginative architect of constitutional progress but whose period as Attorney-General prior to his elevation to the bench was scarcely creditable or even credible in its ferocity and intemperate rhetoric.[3] His judicial career, which was marked by his dismissal as Chief Justice of the Common Pleas in 1613 and his brief career as Chief Justice of the King's Bench 1613–16, which again ended in dismissal, and his post-judicial career linked to the House of Commons were remarkable and ground-breaking; and his writings, especially the *Institutes*, were critical at the start of the constitutional ferment of the 17th century.

In the course of a century when the legal system in this country was by no means stable and when notions of judicial independence were varied and uncertain, Coke succeeded in pointing a new direction with regard to the royal prerogative, to a supreme constitution, to moves towards a bill of rights, to assertions of constitutional judicial review, and ultimately to the securing of a large measure of judicial independence. The immense contrast between Coke pre-1606 and Coke after 1606 is described in these words by Lord Campbell in his *Lives of the Chief Justices*[4]:

> Coke, while Attorney General, was liable to the severest censure; he unscrupulously stretched the prerogative of the Crown, showing himself for the time being utterly regardless of public liberty; he perverted the criminal law to the oppression of many individuals; and the arrogance of his demeanour to all mankind is unparalleled. But he made a noble amends. The whole of his subsequent career is entitled to the highest admiration.

THE ROYAL PREROGATIVE

The royal prerogative was under constant scrutiny throughout the 17th century. Early in his judicial career, in *Prohibitions del Roy*[5] and in the *Case of Proclamations*[6] respectively, the King was obliged to back down over

---

[3] See Catherine Drinker Bowen, *The Lion under the Throne. The Life and Times of Sir Edward Coke 1552–1634* (1957); John Hostettler, *Sir Edward Coke. A Force for Freedom* (1997).

[4] John, Lord Campbell, The Lives of the Chief Justices of England. From the Norman Conquest Till the Death of Lord Tenterden, new and revised edition (James Cockcroft (ed), 1894) Vol 1, 377. This edition was published in the United States.

[5] (1607) 12 Co Rep 63. On Coke's arguments, see AV Dicey, Introduction to the Law of the Constitution (8th edn, 1915) 17–19.

[6] (1611), 12 Co Rep 74. See Catherine Drinker Bowen, *The Lion under the Throne*, above n 3, ch 24.

assertions of power to withdraw cases from the courts for his Majesty's personal determination and over the practice where the King 'began to issue proclamations whenever he thought that the existing law required amendment.'[7] On the latter issue it is worth noting, lest these arguments are relegated to the accidents of history, that the government has this year had to accept many amendments to the Legislative and Regulatory Reform Bill—now enacted—which in its original form allowed the government through delegated legislation to 'rewrite almost any Act and, in some cases, enact new laws that at present only Parliament can make.'[8] In the Second Reading debate in the House of Lords on 13 June 2006, one of their Lordships complained that six 'silly' Cambridge law professors, of whom I was one, had written a letter to *The Times* encouraging an emotional response to the original Bill akin to the hysteria stimulated by the Witches of Salem[9]; but I am content to be one of the Cambridge Six and I believe that Chief Justice Coke would have approved of our early intervention. Other judicial questioning of the old-style royal prerogative continued in the 17th century, with *Hampden's Case* (1637)[10] highlighting the taxation powers of the Crown in times of emergency and *Godden v Hales* (1686)[11] raising the issue of the dispensing power of the Crown. But, even after the close of the century and the effective victory of Parliament, the royal prerogative remained a major and difficult challenge in constitutional law both in relation to foreign affairs and domestic affairs.[12]

Most prerogative powers today are, of course, exercised by the executive, but there are still crucial problems of both judicial and parliamentary control. Over the past 30 years the courts have ruled on several important aspects of the prerogative, in terms of definition and exercise, though there are allied problems of justiciability involved in their rulings.[13] There are also the familiar arguments of judicial restraint as against judicial activism when the government acts in areas of national security and foreign affairs. Yet there is mounting public concern about alleged inadequacy of either judicial or parliamentary control over such decisions as declarations of war,

[7] Lord Campbell, above n 4, 384.

[8] Letter from six Cambridge law professors, *The Times* 16 February 2006, at 18. The letter was drafted by Professor John Spencer QC.

[9] Parl Deb, HL, Vol 683, c 161, 13 June 2006 (Lord Lipsey). See, on the earlier Deregulation and Contracting Out Act 1994, Sir David Williams, 'Subordinate Legislation and Judicial Control' (1997) 8 Public Law Review 77, esp at 78–9.

[10] *R v Hampden* (The Case of Ship-Money) (1637) 3 St Tr 825. See generally, DL Keir and FH Lawson, *Cases in Constitutional Law* (6th edn, FH Lawson and DJ Bentley, 1979) ch 2 ('Prerogative').

[11] (1686) II St Tr 1165. See the earlier case of *Thomas v Sorrell* (1674) Vaughan 330, also on the dispensing power.

[12] See Hilaire Barnett, *Constitutional and Administrative Law* (6th edn, 2006) ch 6 ('The Royal Prerogative').

[13] See HWR Wade and Christopher Forsyth, *Administrative Law* (8th edn, 2000) 348–51. See also, DGT Williams, case-note ('Prerogative-Control') at [1971] CLJ 178–80.

reflected in the decision as to Iraq in 2003[14]; over the granting of honours, reflected in the current controversy over alleged donations or loans to political parties[15]; and in the exercise of the prerogative of mercy, reflected in the lengthy battles over the conviction and execution of Derek Bentley in 1953[16] and more recently in the proposed statutory authorisation of pardons for the many servicemen executed in the First World War on charges such as cowardice or desertion.[17] These are not the sorts of issues faced in the 17th century by Coke and his successors but they are a reminder that the royal prerogative is still an important part of our unwritten constitution and that the courts have an indispensable role in intervening or hovering at the outskirts of various claims of prerogative power. Chief Justice Coke had pointed the way.

A SUPREME CONSTITUTION?

Another area opened up by Coke was that of a supreme constitution, a concept that has been formally denied in this country since the adoption of the doctrine of parliamentary sovereignty in the aftermath of the Glorious Revolution of 1688–89.[18] In the rather more fluid 17th century, Coke turned to and re-invented Magna Carta as a form of fundamental law. Magna Carta was invoked unsuccessfully in *Darnel's Case* in 1629,[19] where the Five Knights attempted to invoke *habeas corpus* after being imprisoned for refusing to pay forced loans to the King. Soon afterwards Coke, now a member of Parliament, was influential in the preparation and adoption of the Petition of Right 1628 that identified a number of grievances—related, for instance, to forced loans, to unjust imprisonment, and to the billeting of soldiers on the people—and 'became symbolic of successful resistance by the Commons against arbitrary royal power.'[20] It is significant that the provision in the Petition of Right against courts martial of civilians in certain circumstances was later to be invoked in the American case of *Ex parte Milligan*[21] in the wake of the Civil War 1861–65 and in a post Second World War challenge to military conviction of civilians in *Duncan*

---

[14] See eg, *R (on the application of the Campaign for Nuclear Disarmament) v Prime Minister* [2002] EWHC 2777 (Admin), DC of QBD.
[15] See *The Times*, 24 August 2006, at 4, reporting the views of the Electoral Commission on loans to political parties.
[16] See *R v Secretary of State for the Home Department, ex p Bentley* [1993] All ER 442 and *R v Bentley* [2001] Cr App R 21.
[17] See *The Times*, 16 August 2006, at 3, *Daily Telegraph*, 16 August 2006, at 1–2.
[18] See JW Gough, *Fundamental Law in English Constitutional History* (1955) 2.
[19] (1627) 3 Howell's St Tr 1.
[20] Arthur E Sutherland, above n 2, at 71. See also, Bernard Schwartz, *The Great Rights of Mankind. A History of the American Bill of Rights* (1977) 8–14.
[21] 4 Wall 2 (1866).

v Kahanamoku.[22] Long ahead of the aftermath of 9/11, Arthur Sutherland of Harvard Law School commented: 'so men still remember it in sorry moments.'[23] The Petition of Right explicitly refers more than once to Magna Carta,[24] and Coke in his remaining years before his death in 1634 was to press home the new emphasis.

Coke's *Second Institute*—on Magna Carta and the Ancient Statutes—was published posthumously in 1642: it had,

> a far-reaching influence upon parliamentarian thought, and numerous references to Coke and the Great Charter can be found in the debates and the statutes of the Long Parliament.[25]

Coke described Magna Carta as 'the fountain of all the fundamental laws of the realm', and there is no doubt that the revival and revised interpretation of Magna Carta at that time did much to bring ideas of fundamental law or a supreme constitution to the forefront of political thought. In the time of Cromwell 1649–58 there was a short-lived written constitution, known as the *Instrument of Government*, which purported to provide a form of fundamental law.[26] At least some of the ideas that later underlaid the federal Constitution of the United States, which came into force in 1789, grew from the constitutional vitality of the 17th century and not least from the inspiration of Sir Edward Coke. The original Magna Carta suffered obsolescence and some measure of repeal in later years, but it continued to be invoked in litigation into the 20th century; and in the recent Belmarsh ruling of the House of Lords on detention without trial, Lord Bingham spoke of,

> the long libertarian tradition of English law, dating back to Ch. 39 of Magna Carta ..., given effect in the ancient remedy of habeas corpus, declared in the Petition of Right ..., upheld in a series of landmark decisions down the centuries and embodied in the substance and procedure of the law to our own day.[27]

---

[22] 327 US 304, 320.

[23] Above n 2, at 72. Both cases (Milligan and Kahanamoku) were referred to in the opinion of the Supreme Court (Stevens J) in the case in 2006 of *Hamdan v Rumsfeld* in which Stevens J referred at one point to 'the seminal case' of ex p Milligan.

[24] Lord Campbell, above n 4, Vol 2, 15.

[25] Anne Pallister, *Magna Carta. The Heritage of Liberty* (1971) 11. See generally, JC Holt, *Magna Carta* (2nd edn, 1992), esp ch 1.

[26] See Theodore FT Plucknett, *A Concise History of the Common Law* (1956) 54: the author described the Instrument of Government as 'a document which purported to be a fundamental constitution which was to be unchangeable save by particularly complicated machinery. This document, therefore, may be properly is a prototype of the written fundamental constitution, as it is known to Americas public law.' See also, Arthur E Sutherland, above n 2, at 79–87 (setting out the text of the Instrument); *Taswell-Langmead English Constitutional History* (11th edn, TFT Plucknett (ed), 1960) 416–17.

[27] *A v Secretary of State for the Home Department* [2005] 3 All ER 169, 195, HL. See casenote by David Feldman, [2005] 64 CLJ 271–3.

A BILL OF RIGHTS

The Petition of Right was one of the leading precursors of the Bill of Rights adopted in England in 1689 and in the United States of the adoption of the first ten Amendments to the Constitution in 1791. Roscoe Pound wrote[28] approvingly of the Petition of Right,

> which with Magna Carta, the Bill of Rights, the Declaration of Independence, and the Constitution of the United States stands as one of the monuments of Anglo-American free institutions.

The Bill of Rights of 1689, which followed on the abdication of James II, took the formulation of rights into[29] a new dimension altogether. To some 18th century Americans it was 'that second Magna Carta' and some of its provisions as well as its title that anticipated the American Bill of Rights of 1791. In years to come there nevertheless remained a strong British reluctance to accept declarations of rights as fundamental law, demonstrated, as Stanley de Smith put it, in Dicey's 'delicate observation' that 'most foreign constitution-makers have begun with declarations of rights. For this they have been in no wise to blame.'[30] In the course of time international and national laws helped to modify that stance with, in particular, such documents as the Universal Declaration of Human Rights and then the European Convention for the Protection of Human Rights and Fundamental Freedoms in the vanguard of changed assumptions and approaches. For the United Kingdom, which had long subscribed to the European Convention, the significant move forward was the incorporation into domestic law of the European Convention by virtue of the Human Rights Act 1998.

Adjudication under the Human Rights Act has undoubtedly brought the judiciary into an unprecedented position with regard to parliament and especially the executive. The Belmarsh decision, reached by an 8–1 majority in the House of Lords, dramatised some of the tensions, as did the decision of the Court of Appeal—consisting of the Lord Chief Justice, the Master of the Rolls and the President of the Queen's Bench Division—at the beginning of August 2006 upholding earlier rulings by Mr Justice Sullivan that six control orders made under the Prevention of Terrorism Act 2005 were in violation of Article 5 of the European Convention.[31] The problems are unlikely to lessen, in the context of anti-terrorist executive action and in other areas such as administrative law, and the courts are likely to remain active despite

---

[28] *The Development of Constitutional Guarantees of Liberty* (1957) at 47. See also, Arthur E Sutherland, above n 2, at 67–8.

[29] See Barnard Schwartz, *The Great Rights of Mankind*, above n 20, at 21.

[30] SA de Smith, *The New Commonwealth and its Constitutions* (1964) 164.

[31] *Secretary of State for the Home Department* (2006) TLR 64. See generally, David Feldman, 'Human Rights, Terrorism and Risk: The Roles of Politicians and Judges' [2006] PL 364.

formal subordination to parliamentary sovereignty. Lord Falconer, the Lord Chancellor, was obliged in May of this year to emphasise that the United Kingdom's commitment to human rights was permanent, and he added[32] that we,

> must be careful, in this debate and in the way we construct a response, to ensure that the independence of the judges is not undermined.

Sir Edward Coke, concerned at least from 1606 about the claims of the executive, would have been astonished to see how far we have progressed from the Petition of Right.

CONSTITUTIONAL JUDICIAL REVIEW

Coke would perhaps have readily explored the potential for judicial review of parliamentary as well as executive action. During his judicial career there was no recognised constitution, there was no doctrine of parliamentary sovereignty, and there was no precedent one way or the other as to the possibility of constitutional judicial review. In 1610 Coke, as Chief Justice of the Common Pleas, provided a precedent of sorts in *Dr Bonham's Case*.[33] In the course of this action for false imprisonment against the censors or governors of the Royal College of Physicians, the claim was made that,

> it appears in our books ... that the common law will control acts of parliament, and sometimes adjudge them to be utterly void, for when an act of parliament is against common right or reason, or repugnant, or impossible to be performed, the common law will control it and adjudge such act to be void.

The interpretation of that claim has never been agreed but it nonetheless furnished a form of words that was destined, in one scholar's view, to become 'the most important single source of the notion of judicial review.'[34] The idea of judicial review did, even in English law, achieve some momentum through *Hampden's Case*,[35] which carried with it judicial comments about inseparable prerogatives that even parliament could not take away.[36] Judicial review was not provided for in the US Constitution of 1789 but it

---

[32] Lord Falconer's comments were at a meeting of the Hansard Society in London: see *The Guardian*, 17 May 2006, at 14.

[33] (1610) 8 Co Rep 118a, See Edward S Corwin, *The 'Higher Law' Background of American Constitutional Law* (originally in the *Harvard Law Review*, reprinted separately 1955); TFT Plucknett, 'Bonham's Case and Judicial Review' (1926) 40 *Harvard Law Review* 30; SE Thorne, 'Dr Bonham's Case' (1938) 54 *LQR* 543; Raoul Berger, 'Dr Bonham's Case: Statutory Construction or Constitutional Theory' (1969) 117 *University of Pennsylvania Law Review* 521; Catherine Drinker Bowen, above n 6, at ch 23.

[34] See Edward S Corwin, above n 33, at 57.

[35] (1637) 3 St Tr 825.

[36] See Keir and Lawson, above n 10, at 81–95, esp at 93–4.

was assumed by Chief Justice Marshall who stressed in *Marbury v Madison* that a supreme constitution must prevail over ordinary legislation and that to deny to the courts a power of judicial review would be 'to overthrow in fact what was established in theory': otherwise we would be 'prescribing limits and declaring that those limits may be passed at pleasure.'[37]

Judicial review of primary or parliamentary legislation, of course, is not an American concern alone, despite the assertion in 1919 by Albert J Beveridge, the major biographer of John Marshall, that the supremacy of written constitutions over legislative acts 'is wholly and exclusively American. It is America's original contribution to the science of law.'[38] In more recent times we have seen, for instance, the brave though ultimately unsuccessful efforts of the Appellate Division of the Supreme Court of South Africa to assert a version of constitutional judicial review in the early days of apartheid. The so-called *Harris* cases[39] attracted immense attention in the early 1950s, and there was considerable interest among American lawyers including Dean Griswold of the Harvard Law School.[40] The rulings of the Appellate Division did not match *Marbury v Madison*, principally because of the different constitutional framework against which they were formulated; but the underlying issues of constitutional judicial review continued to be raised and explored, in New Zealand through the judicial comments of Sir Robin Cooke, as he then was, who in one case[41] declared,

> that it is arguable that some common law rights may go so deep that even Parliament cannot be accepted by the Courts to have destroyed them

and in England through the extra-judicial comments of Lord Woolf[42] to the effect that,

> ultimately there are even limits on the supremacy of Parliament which it is the courts' inalienable responsibility to identify and uphold.

---

[37] I Cranch 137, 177–8 (1803).

[38] *The Life of John Marshall*, Vol 111, *Conflict and Construction* (1919) 142.

[39] *Harris v Minister of the Interior* [1952] 2 South African LR 428; *Minister of the Interior v Harris* [1952] 2 South African LR 769. See Geoffrey Marshall, *Parliamentary Sovereignty and the Commonwealth* (1957) Part 3, ch XI ('South Africa: The Courts and the Constitution') at 139–248; CF Forsyth, *In Danger for their Talents. A Study of the Appellate Division of the Supreme Court of South Africa from 1950–80* (1985) 61–74; E McWhinney, 'The Union Parliament, the Supreme Court, and the "Entrenched Clauses" of the South Africa Act' (1952) 30 *Canadian Bar Review* 692 (see also articles by McWhinney at (1952) 30 *Canadian Bar Review* 734 and (1954) 32 *Canadian Bar Review* 44; DV Cowen, 'Legislature and Judiciary: Reflections on the Constitutional Issues in South Africa' (1952) 15 *MLR* 282 and (1953) 16 *MLR* 273.

[40] Erwin N Griswold, *Ould Fields, New Corne. The Personal Memoirs of a Twentieth Century Lawyer* (1992) 201–3; 'The 'Coloured Vote Case' in South Africa' (1952) 65 *Harvard Law Review* 1361; 'The Demise of the High Court of Parliament in South Africa' (1953) 66 *Harvard Law Review* 864.

[41] *Fraser v State Services Commission* [1984] 1 NZLR 116, 121, CA. See also Cooke J in *Taylor v New Zealand Poultry Board* [1984] 1 NZLR 394, 398.

[42] Lord Woolf of Barnes, 'Droit Public-English Style' [1995] *PL* 57, 69.

Moreover the views of Lord Woolf have been given a robust expression in the context of European law and parliamentary sovereignty by the late Sir William Wade,[43] who saw the *Factortame* litigation[44] as offering,[45]

> a further example of the constitution bending before the winds of change as in the last resort it will always succeed in doing.

Once again Sir Edward Coke would have welcomed the sustained vitality of his words in *Dr Bonham's Case*.

JUDICIAL INDEPENDENCE

Coke's contribution to the cause of judicial independence is more problematical, but his own experiences were an early reminder of the increasing anomalies in the 17th century that stemmed from the absence of what we now take for granted in assessments of independent and stable judicial systems. Coke himself was dismissed as Chief Justice of the Common Pleas in 1613 after one of many disputes with the King, but in October of the same year he re-emerged as Chief Justice of the King's Bench. However, disputes with the King continued, and in November 1616 he was dismissed as Chief Justice of the King's Bench, not without being reminded by one correspondent[46] that in discourse,

> you delight to speak too much, not to hear other men; this, some say, becomes a pander, not a Judge, for by this sometimes your affections are intangled with a love of your own arguments though they be the weaker ...

The vulnerability of judges persisted through the 17th century, at least during the royalist years, and the independence of the judiciary was severely prejudiced. George Keeton once observed[47] that during the 17th century the,

> judiciary became drawn into the political struggle, and regrettably, but nevertheless inevitably, justice in state trials became political action disguised by judicial forms.

And another commentator has observed that 'politics and law were more closely associated under the Stuarts than at any other time in modern

---

[43] HWR Wade, 'Sovereignty—Revolution or Evolution' (1996) 112 *LQR* 568, 573.
[44] See esp *R v Secretary of State for Transport, ex p Factortame Ltd (No 2)* [1991] 1 AC 603, HL.
[45] Above n 43, at 575.
[46] Quoted from manuscript sources by John Hostettler, above n 3, at 93–4.
[47] GW Keeton, *Lord Chancellor Jeffreys and the Stuart Course* (1965) 94. See also, GW Keeton, 'The Judiciary and the Constitutional Struggle, 1680–88' (1962) VII *Journal of the SPTL* 56.

English history.'[48] Despite particularly strong royal manipulation of the judiciary in the later years of Charles II's reign—which was carried over into the reign of James II 1685–88[49]—there were limits, and even a royalist judge, Sir Thomas Jones, who was Chief Justice of the Common Pleas, lost office when he declined to bend to James II's wishes on the dispensing power ahead of the decision in *Godden v Hales* (1686).[50]

Insecurity of tenure ensured during this period that many judges were strong supporters of the monarchy; and many lawyers, often looking to elevation to the bench, were likewise strong supporters.

The Glorious Revolution marked the beginning of a new constitutional climate, however, and by the end of the century the time was ripe for some measure of statutory endorsement of the new settlement. This came about in the Act of Settlement 1701 which, as Robert Stevens has pointed out,[51] was in part a statement of Parliament's frustrations in the immediate aftermath of the Glorious Revolution. It provided for the line of succession to the throne and it also provided that the judges' commissions should be 'made *quamdice se bene gesserint* and that the judges' salaries should be 'ascertained and established', adding judges could lawfully be removed 'upon the address of both Houses of Parliament.' The victory was not immediate, but the ground had been laid for wide acceptance of the desirability of, indeed the necessity for, judicial independence, not least with regard to casual dismissals of judges. Once again Sir Edward Coke would have approved, and the early Jamestown settlers might have been astonished at the constitutional turmoil that enveloped their homeland during the 17th century and at the constitutional legacy of judicial decisions such as *Dr Bonham's Case* and *Godden v Hales*, of legislative measures such as the Petition of Right and the Bill of Rights, of the Civil War and the *Instrument of Government*, and of the Act of Settlement itself allowing scope for the establishment of an instinctive respect for the rule of law.

The emphasis to this point has largely been upon England and upon the United States, pre-independence and post-independence. It goes without saying that independent and stable judicial systems are desirable, though not always achieved in all countries that claim to be democratic. In a Report entitled *The Rule of Law in a Free Society*, which emerged from

---

[48] AP Havinghurst, 'The Judiciary and Politics in the Reign of Charles II' (1950) 66 *LQR* 62, 229, at 250.

[49] AP Havinghurst, 'James II and the Twelve Men in Scarlet' (1953) 69 *LQR* 522.

[50] See GW Keeton, above n 47, at 64–5 of the article in the *Journal of the SPTL*. In the *Oxford DNB* David Yale cites a description of Jones as 'a very reverend and learned judge, a gentleman, and impartial, but being of Welsh extraction was apt to be warm ...' On Judge Jeffreys—see a fascinating article by Lord Oliver of Aylmerton, *A Very Ill Man* in (1989–90) 14 *Holdsworth Law Review* 1–15.

[51] *The English Judges. Their Role in the Changing Constitution* (2002) 8.

the International Congress of Jurists in New Delhi in 1959, it is stated that in,

> a free society, whether it has a written constitution or not and whether or not this constitution is subject to the review of a judicial body, the position of the Judiciary and the individual judges is of special importance,

but it is added[52] that to,

> assert the independence of the Judiciary ... is even in free societies to state an ideal rather than a fully realized condition of fact.

In the relevant part of the Report it sets out areas where practice can vary greatly from one jurisdiction to another: in the selection of judges, in the participation of the lay element in the judiciary, in the promotion of judges, in the dismissal and compulsory retirement of judges, and in the security or maintenance of the judicial system.[53] Changes in all these areas occur from time to time, of course, and this country is currently adjusting to the establishment in the near future of a Supreme Court in place of the Appellate Committee of the House of Lords, and to the setting up of a Judicial Appointments Commission. The office of Lord Chancellor has been changed out of recognition,[54] thus ending a 'dual existence' as a politician on the one hand and the head of the judges and our judicial system on the other.[55] In other words the office of Lord Chancellor ceased to be embraced by the principle adopted by the Royal Commission on the Constitution after its examination over 30 years ago of the constitutional standing of the Channel Islands and the Isle of Man[56], namely that,

> anomalies... should be, if not encouraged, at least accepted so long as they are cherished by those most directly affected and do no harm to others.

Given the transformed constitutional standing of the courts of law in the United Kingdom in recent years—through the impact of membership of the

---

[52] International Commission of Jurists, *The Rule of Law in a Free Society. A Report on the International Congress of Jurists* (1959) (prepared by Norman S Marsh) 279.

[53] *Ibid*, at 281–95.

[54] See, in particular, the Constitutional Reform Act 2005. See also, Lord Cooke of Thorndon, 'The Law Lords: an Endangered Heritage' (2003) 119 *LQR* 49; Lord Steyn, 'The Case for a Supreme Court' (2002) 118 *LQR* 382; Lord Hope of Craighead, 'A Phoenix from the Ashes? Accommodating a New Supreme Court' (2005) 121 *LQR* 253; Lord Bingham, 'The Old Order Changeth' (2006) 122 *LQR* 211; Diana Woodhouse, 'Judges and the Lord Chancellor in the changing United Kingdom Constitution: Independence and Accountability' (2005) *Public Law Review* 227; Lord Bingham of Cornhill, 'The Old Order Changeth' (2006) 122 *LQR* 211.

[55] See Parl Deb, HL, Vol 572, cc 1262 and 1269 (Lord Renton and Lord Mishcon); and see also, Diana Woodhouse, 'The Office of Lord Chancellor' [1998] *PL* 617.

[56] Report of the Royal Commission on the Constitution 1969–1973, Cmnd 5460, para 1460.

European Union, through the explosion of judicial review of administrative action over the past 30 to 40 years, through the impact of devolutionary legislation, and through the Human Rights Act 1998—it is perhaps useful to itemise the likely effect on independence and stability considered on the basis of experience in this country and selectively on the basis of experience in other comparable countries that seek to adhere to ideals of the rule of law. It is surely legitimate to speak of judicial review even where there is no supreme constitution since what we are most concerned with is the interrelationship between the judicial system, the legislature and the executive in an attempt to assess the democratically acceptable role for the courts of law.

This process of itemisation can highlight the dependence of judicial review on litigation; an alleged excess of legalism in government; the need for the courts constantly to avoid over-extending their role; the inevitability nevertheless of some judicial involvement in the political arena; and the special demands of judicial independence when the courts exercise or approach the exercise of constitutional judicial review, a topic that includes the appointment, tenure, remuneration and removal of judges. I am acutely aware of the extensive writing of so many judges, lawyers, academic lawyers and politicians on these sorts of issues,[57] and all I can hope to do is highlight the implications of recent developments against some of the lessons and precedents of the Anglo-American 17th century.

Dependence on Litigation

To speak, in the context of judicial review, of dependence on litigation is to remind us that there is a strong element of chance involved. James Bradley Thayer once wrote[58] that it,

> is only as litigation may spring up, and as the course of it may happen to raise the point of constitutionality, that any questions for the courts can regularly emerge. It may be, then, that the mere legislative decision will accomplish results throughout the country of the profoundest importance before any judicial question can arise or be decided ...

---

[57] See esp the writings of Robert Stevens, the latest of which is *The English Judges. Their Role in the Changing Constitution* (2002). See also his *The Independence of the Judiciary. The View from the Lord Chancellor's Office* (1993). On a comparative common law theme, reference should be made to Enid Campbell and HP Lee, *The Australian Judiciary* (2001); Martin L Friedland, *A Place Apart: Judicial Independence and Accountability in Canada*. A Report to the Canadian Judicial Council (1995); WR Lederman, 'The Independence of the Judiciary' (1956) 34 *Canadian Bar Review* 769, 1139. See also, S Shetreet, *Judges on Trial* (1976). BD Gray and RB McClintock, *Courts and Policy. Checking the Balance* (1995).

[58] *Legal Essays* (1908): 'The Origin and Scope of the American Doctrine of Constitutional Law' at 1–41, at 9–10. This paper or chapter was originally delivered to the Congress on Jurisprudence and Law Reform at the World's Fair in Chicago in August 1893 and was later reprinted in (1893–94) 7 *Harvard Law Review* 129.

In effect this means, as Thayer sees it, that there is no all-embracing scheme of judicial supervision of constitutionality, and many unhappy phases of legislative, executive or public activity can occur without the courts having the opportunity or rejecting the opportunity to intervene.

The element of chance can be illustrated by reference to events in the United States in the 1950s. On the one hand there was the unanimous decision of the Supreme Court in *Brown v Board of Education*,[59] handed down on 17 May 1954, which—even allowing for the enormous and still applicable problems of implementation yet to come—was in its rejection of racial segregation one of the greatest of all contributions to constitutional jurisprudence anywhere or at any time. The 40th anniversary of the case led to the comment in *The Washington Post*[60] that seldom had a ruling of the Supreme Court had,

> such a profound impact on the country's social structure, moral tone or constitutional assumptions as to become a benchmark event in the nation's history.

I was privileged to be present at the 50th anniversary celebrations organised by the American Law Institute in Washington DC in 2004.

Amid the euphoria that greeted the *Brown* decision in 1954, however, there was, on the other hand, still the closing chapter of McCarthyism to be brought to an end. The Supreme Court had played only a subsidiary role, if at all, in resistance to the excesses of the junior senator from Wisconsin from 1950, and in 1954 three separate events—which involved lawyers from time to time—but not judges—finally sounded the death-knell of a strange hysteria in American political life. In the first of these events, Dean Erwin Griswold of Harvard Law School delivered an after-dinner speech in early February to the Massachusetts Bar Association that gave vent to his annoyance,

> that no one in the law school world throughout the country was speaking out against the tactics of the McCarthyites,

especially with regard to the privilege against self-incrimination enshrined in the Fifth Amendment of the Constitution.'[61] The second event, which became the centrepiece of a film called *Good Night, and Good Luck* directed by George Clooney and released in October 2005, was a famous

---

[59] 347 US 483 (1954). See Richard Kluger, *Simple Justice* (1976). With reference to the 'separate but equal' doctrine set out in *Plessy v Ferguson* 163 US 637 (1896), see Charles A Lofgreen, *The Plessy Case. A Legal-Historical Interpretation* (1987).

[60] 17 May 1994, at A16. See also, the *New York Times*, 18 May 1994, at A22, which took a rather less encouraging view, commenting that 'it seems the national consciousness has changed but the reality lags far behind'. See Bernard Schwartz, *Swann's Way. The School Busing Case and the Supreme Court* (1986). See the Report of the American Law Institute setting out the Remarks and Addresses on 17 May 2004.

[61] Erwin N Griswold, *Ould Fields, New Corne*, above n 40, at 192–4.

'See it Now' programme broadcast by Edward R Murrow on 9 March 1954 directly attacking Senator McCarthy and reminding us that the fault, dear Brutus, lies not in our stars but in ourselves. It was a devastating performance.[62] The third event consisted of the hearings before a Senate committee on McCarthy's allegations against the Army heard between April and June 1954. The Army's special counsel at the hearings was Joseph N Welch, a 63-year-old Boston lawyer, who finally destroyed McCarthy with the words 'Have you no decency, sir, at long last? Have you no sense of decency?' The climate in the country had changed radically, in no time a conservative Republican congressman declared that,

> McCarthyism has become a synonym for witch-hunting, star-chamber methods, and the denial of those civil liberties which have distinguished our country in its historic growth,

and the Senate censured McCarthy in a vote of 67 to 22.[63] Joseph Welch went on to star as the judge in his only film, *Anatomy of a Murder* (1959), before his death in 1960.

That recitation of events of 1954, following on a long period of McCarthyism, brings to mind the comment of Justice Robert H Jackson of the Supreme Court (1941–54)—who controversially had stepped down temporarily in 1945–46 to be the chief prosecutor at Nuremberg—that it,

> is not idle speculation to inquire which comes first, either in time or importance, an independent and enlightened judiciary or a free and tolerant society.

He added that it was his,[64]

> belief that the attitude of a society and of its organized political forces, rather than its legal machinery, is the controlling force in the character of free institutions.

He also said that he knew,[65]

> of no modern instance in which any judiciary has saved a whole people from the great currents of intolerance, passion, usurpation, and tyranny which have threatened liberty and free institutions.

Some years later, after an analysis of the affirmative role of the courts after *Brown v Board of Education*, Archibald Cox—in the Chichele Lectures

---

[62] See Alexander Kendrick, *Prime Time. The Life of Edward R Murrow* (1970) ch 2 ('The terror is right here in this room').

[63] See William Manchester, *The Glory and the Dream. A Narrative History of America 1932–1972* (1974) ch 21 ('Mr Chairman, Mr Chairman'); David Halberstam, *The Fifties* (1993) ch 3 which begins (in 1950) with the words at p 49: 'The McCarthy era was about to begin'; Richard H Rovere, *Senator McCarthy* (1959).

[64] Robert H Jackson. *The Supreme Court in the American System of Government* (1955) 81.

[65] *Ibid*, at 80.

delivered at Oxford University in 1975—spoke of the school desegregation decrees issued by the federal courts and declared that,[66]

> approval of the aim and even of the means chosen should not blind us either to the novel aspects of the judicial venture or to the resulting degree of judicial dependence upon political support. The courts cannot possibly go it alone.

Legalism in Government

The second itemised factor on judicial review brings us to what might be called the other side of the coin. There is from time to time an undue reliance on the courts and an undue legalism in government as a result. Dicey saw federal government, for instance, as encouraging legalism, a term that he defined as 'the predominance of the judiciary in the constitution.'[67] Whatever the definition should be, it is worthy of note that in the wake of what one observer described as the 'geometric pace' of developments in English administrative law combined with 'a quantum change in the judicial role',[68] the Treasury Solicitor's Department issued a booklet in 1967 entitled *The Judge Over Your Shoulder* now in its 4th edition from January 2006. This booklet recognises an increased willingness on the part of the judiciary to question acts of the executive, implicitly warning civil servants to anticipate and adjust their procedures and style to meet possible legal challenge.[69] Yet even if open, to some extent, to the charge of encouraging a legalistic approach among public servants at central or local level, it may be a happy outcome for the courts if, for instance, the reasons for administrative decisions were to be clear and full and if consultation required by statute were to be genuine, open and comprehensive.

There is no doubt that some individual decisions of the courts stand out in public law as warnings of objections to particular practices or prejudices. In this country, *Entick v Carrington* (1765), in its ruling on general warrants, is an outstanding example[70]; in the United States *Brown v Board of Education* (1954) remains a beacon in the rejection of racial discrimination.[71] It might have been preferable, however, if the courts had insisted in some situations on greater propriety, whether it is seen as an emphasis on legality or legalism or simple fairness, in both legislative and especially executive responses. This is especially true in wartime or in emergency

[66] Archibald Cox, *The Role of the Supreme Court in American Government* (1976) 77–90 ('School Desegregation') 88. See also, Archibald Cox, *The Warren Court. Constitutional Decision as an Instrument of Reform* (1968), esp ch 2.
[67] Dicey, *Law of the Constitution*, above n 5, at ch 3, p 170.
[68] Bernard Schwartz, (1995) 44 *Administrative Law* at 75 and 81.
[69] See the comments of Lord Borrie in Parl Deb, HL, Vol 572, LC 1292–3, 5 June 1996. The new edition of *JOYS* has a preface by the Cabinet Secretary, Sir Gus O'Donnell.
[70] (1765) 19 St Tr 1029.
[71] Above n 59.

situations such as that created by the current waves of terrorism throughout the world. Wartime decisions have not been easy, whether or not the courts had exercised full powers of judicial review under a supreme constitution— as shown by experience of British and American law in both world wars and sometimes in the aftermath of war.[72] The threat of terrorism has already led to a stream of books, articles and conferences; and, in addition, the response of some courts has been fascinating and encouraging.[73] This is an area which I would wish to explore at length, and perhaps I will do so in a lecture on the occasion of the 450th anniversary of the Jamestown settlement. It is, however, important to recognise the long-term impact for the administration and the legislature of judicial decisions that are in their turn bolstered by a supreme constitution or by the impact of a Human Rights Act or by the explosion in administrative law. Arthur Sutherland once wrote on the American position in terms which can be adapted to many democratic countries[74]:

> The effect of judicial review on national legislation is not limited to those cases in which congressional enactments are declared invalid. The possibility of future judgments of unconstitutionality may have an inhibitory advance effect on legislators, either in producing opposition on the floor, or so shaping legislation as to avoid constitutional difficulties.

Judicial Restraint

The third itemised factor in considering judicial review is that the courts need constantly to advert to the desirable or permissible limits of their function. This raises the familiar topic of judicial restraint, familiar enough in administrative law in this country but now relevant in a wider constitutional context. In administrative law, Mr Justice Richardson once voiced his concern, in a dissenting judgment of the Court of Appeal in New Zealand, about 'the constitutional and democratic implications of judicial involvement in wider issues of public policy and public interest',[75] an approach

---

[72] See eg Zechariah Chafee, Jr, *Free Speech in the United States* (1941) replacing his *Freedom of Speech* (1920); William Preston, Jr, *Aliens and Dissenters. Federal Suppression of Radicals, 1903–1933* (1963); Clinton Rossiter, *Constitutional Dictatorship. Crisis Government in the Modern Democracies* (1948); AWB Simpson, *In the Highest Degree Odious: Detention without Trial in Wartime Britain* (1992).

[73] See generally, Conor Gearty, *Can Human Rights Survive?* (2006) (The Hamlyn Lectures 2005). See also, Dame Mary Arden, 'Human rights in the Age of Terrorism' (2005) 121 *LQR* 604.

[74] *Constitutionalism in America*, above n 2, at 336.

[75] *Petrocorp Exploration Ltd v Minister of Energy* [1991] 1 NZLR 1, 46, CA. The case concerned a minister's discretion in the award of licences for oil exploration. The decision of the Court of Appeal was overturned by the Judicial Committee of the Privy Council at [1991] 1 NZLR 641, PC.

echoed in an English case by Master of the Rolls Sir Thomas Bingham, as he then was, who said[76] that the,

> greater the policy content of a decision, and the more remote the subject matter of a decision from ordinary judicial experience, the more hesitant the court must necessarily be ...

A particularly strong assertion of the need for judicial restraint was that of Lord Mustill, dissenting in the House of Lords, who said in the course of his speech that it is 'the task of Parliament and the executive in tandem, not of the courts, to govern the country.'[77]

Whatever the constitutional context, the advocates of judicial restraint are frequently the more eloquent, though not necessarily the more convincing. The underlying issues are those of justiciability,[78] the appropriate democratic role of the courts,[79] particular factors in this country such as the impact of the convention of ministerial responsibility[80] or the concept of benevolent interpretation of local government decisions,[81] and doubtless special factors—such as a federal-state constitutional structure in other countries.[82] Often there is a balance to be struck, as when Archibald Cox—facing the arguments for judicial restraint put forward by the likes of Judge Leonard Hand—claimed[83] that constitutional adjudication in the United States,

> depends ... upon a delicate, symbiotic relation ... The aspirations voiced by the Court must be those the community is willing not only to avow but in the end to live by.

Sometimes the assertions of judicial restraint can be strong and controversial, as in the address given by Justice Dyson Heydon some months ahead of his elevation to the High Court of Australia in 2002.[84] In the course of

---

[76] *R v Ministry of Defence, ex p Smith* [1966] 1 All ER 257, 264–6, CA. The case concerned homosexuals in the armed forces.

[77] *R v Home Secretary, ex p Fire Brigades Union* [1995] 2 AC 513, 567–8, HL.

[78] See eg, DGT Williams, 'Justiciability and the Control of Discretionary Power' in Michael Taggart (ed), *Judicial Review of Administrative Action in the 1980s* (1987) 103–22.

[79] See eg, J Skelly Wright, 'The Role of the Supreme Court in a Democratic Society—Judicial Activism or Restraint' (1968) 54 *Cornell Law Review* 1; Jeremy Waldron, 'Compared to What? Judicial Activism and New Zealand in Parliament' (2005) *New Zealand Law Journal*, 409.

[80] See eg, *Liversidge v Anderson* (1941) 3 All ER 378, at 346–7 (Lord Maugham) and 378 (Lord Wright) and *Point of Ayr Collieries v Lloyd George* [1943] 2 All ER 546–7 (Lord Greene MR).

[81] See eg *Kruse v Johnson* [1898] 2 QB 91, 99 (Lord Russell of Killowen CJ). See Sir David Williams, 'Subordinate Legislation and Judicial Control' (1997) 8 *Public Law Review* 77, at 83–5.

[82] See eg the Hon Justice Potter Stewart, 'Robert H Jackson's Influence on Federal-State Relationships' in *Justice Jackson. Four Lectures in his Honour* (1969) 57–86, esp at 84–6.

[83] *The Role of the Supreme Court in American Government*, above n 66, at 117–18.

[84] Dyson Heydon, 'Judicial Activism and the Death of the Rule of Law, *Quadrant*, January–February 2003, at 9–22. The address was delivered to a Quadrant dinner in Sydney on 30 October 2002. For some of the initial reaction to Justice Heydon's elevation, see the *Sydney Morning Herald*, 18 December 2002, at 3 and 19 December 2002, at 8; *The Australian*, 18 December 2002, at 1. See also, Justice JD Heydon, 'Limits to the Powers of Ultimate Appellate Courts' (2006) *LQR* 399.

his address he spoke of the differing approach in common law and constitutional law of Sir Owen Dixon and Sir Anthony Mason as Chief Justices of Australia, and he argued that the,

> more the courts freely change the law, the more the public will come to view their function as political; the more they would rightly be open to vigorous and direct public attack on political grounds; and the greater will be the demand for public hearings into the politics of judicial candidates before appointment and greater control over judicial behaviour of the appointment.[85]

That statement alone should ensure continuing debate.

Judges and Politics

Some judicial intrusion in the political process is inevitable, however, and this is the lesson of my fourth itemised point. With regard to Australia, in a case which involved Section 92 of the Constitution (the 'commerce clause') in the context of banking, the Judicial Committee affirmed the High Court and Lord Porter conceded[86] that the problem to be solved under Section 92,

> will often be not so much legal as political, social, or economic, yet it must be solved by a court of law.

Soon afterwards the High Court by 6 to 1 ruled in *The Australian Communist Party v The Commonwealth*[87] that the Communist Party Dissolution Act 1950 was invalid, a decision which one commentator has described as 'probably the most important ever rendered by the High Court' through,

> its confirmation of fundamental constitutional principles such as the rule of law, its impact on civil liberties, its symbolic importance as a reaffirmation of judicial independence, and its political impact.[88]

It is significant today that Mr Justice Williams, one of the majority in the High Court, said that such legislation,

> can only be valid in times of grave crisis during hostilities waged on a large scale, and it must, even then, be limited to such preventive steps as are reasonably necessary to protect the nation during the crisis.[89]

---

[85] *Quadrant*, above n 84, at 22.

[86] *Commonwealth of Australia v Bank of New South Wales* [1950] AC 235, 310, PC. See Peter Johnstone, 'The Bank Nationalisation Cases: The Defect of Labor's Most Controversial Economic Initiative' in HP Lee and George Winterton (eds), *Australian Constitutional Landmarks* (2003) ch 4.

[87] (1951) 83 CLR 1.

[88] George Winterton, 'The Communist Party Case' in *Australian Constitutional Landmarks*, above n 86, ch 5, at 129.

[89] (1951) 83 CLR at 227.

The Canadian courts have also been involved in political controversy, as in the 6–3 decision of the Supreme Court in the 'patriation' controversy over the Canadian constitution in 1981.[90] There was also the issue of the position of Quebec and possible secession from Canada when the Supreme Court in 1998 was obliged to consider 'momentous questions that go to the heart of our system of constitutional government.'[91] The British courts have, as we have seen, become embroiled in the context of international and domestic terrorism, and the political impact of the Human Rights Act is likely to increase. Much more familiar with political controversy are the federal courts of the United States—in the battles during the New Deal over the commerce clause of the federal Constitution which led President Roosevelt at one point to consider enlarging and packing the Supreme Court[92]; in the battles over racial desegregation and over civil liberties under the Warren Court[93]; and generally in many of the most critical and sensitive areas of government action and public policy.[94]

One of the consequences of judicial involvement in sensitive areas of public policy is that the judiciary on occasion becomes the target of political attack. Even ministers can launch attacks on the courts in general or in the wake of particular decisions, and the judges have on occasion asserted a right of reply. In 1997, for instance, the former Chief Justice of Australia, Sir Anthony Mason, spoke of,

> criticisms which were damaging public confidence in the court, criticisms that in my view reflected a lamentable failure to respect the independence of the judiciary and a failure to appreciate the importance of the rule of law as a central pillar in our society.

This was followed by a serving member of the High Court, Justice Michael Kirby, who, while accepting measured criticisms, strongly objected to excessive responses, claiming that he had 'seen countries where the power of the courts has been eroded by unrelenting political attacks.'[95] It is difficult, of course, to avoid criticism of the judiciary in public statements and

---

[90] *Reference re amendment of the Constitution of Canada (Nos 1, 2 and 3)* (1981) 125 DLR (3) 1. For an entertaining account of the background, see Pierre Trudeau, *Memoirs* (1993) Part 4.

[91] *Re Reference by the Governor in Council concerning certain questions relating to the secession of Quebec from Canada* (1998) 161 DLR (4th) 385, 393.

[92] See Robert H Jackson, *The Struggle for Judicial Supremacy. A Study of a Crisis in American Power Politics* (1941).

[93] See Bernard Schwartz, *Super Chief. Earl Warren and his Supreme Court—A Judicial Biography* (1983).

[94] See William H Rehnquist, *The Supreme Court* (1987), in the course of which he discusses the court-packing plan and the steel seizure case under President Truman; Mark Tushnet, *Taking the Constitution away from the Courts* (1999).

[95] *The Sydney Morning Herald*, 16 August 1997, at 1 and 17. See also editorial comment at 18.

speeches, in the newspapers and on television, and on the internet; and in the United States there is often loud and sustained criticism about judicial decisions. The judges themselves, in speeches and addresses outside court, have done much to ensure more balanced debate, and it is the responsibility of ministers, politicians and the judiciary itself to steer clear of invective and intemperate remarks. Only as a last resort would the judges be tempted to invoke or revive that curious species of criminal contempt of court known as contempt by scandalising the court, but there can be variations of approach from one jurisdiction to another.[96]

CONCLUSIONS

Variations in approach are inevitable when we turn, as my final point, to judicial independence in general. Judicial independence has attracted an enormous literature and from time to time it erupts in the context of particular controversies. These controversies include dramatic events such as that in Malaysia in 1988, which included the removal from office of the Lord President of the Supreme Court of Malaysia,[97] and the protracted attack on the federal judiciary in the early years of Thomas Jefferson's presidency, culminating in the unsuccessful impeachment of Associate Justice Samuel Chase 1804 that marked what has been called one 'of the few really great crises in American history.'[98] The appointment of judges can obviously raise issues of judicial independence, not least in the United States where the process of nomination of federal judges—especially those relating to the Supreme Court—and the final requirement of approval by the Senate can bring out issues of competence, of integrity, of geographical origins, of the need for women to be appointed or for some minority groups to be represented, and, of course, of political inclinations. It is well known that the first non-white person appointed to the Supreme Court was Thurgood Marshall in 1967, the first woman was Sandra Day O'Connor in 1981, the first Roman Catholic was Chief Justice Roger B Taney in 1836, and the first Jewish member was Louis D Brandeis in 1916.[99] The first Jewish nominee, it might be noticed, was Judah P Benjamin in 1853, but he declined the nomination in favour of continuing as a senator, later serving in the Confederate cabinet of Jefferson Davis and then escaping to England. There

[96] See *Ambard v Attorney General for Trinidad and Tobago* [1936] AC 322, 335, PC, *R v Dunbabin, ex p Williams* (1935) 53 CLR 434, 443, High Court of Australia.

[97] See HP Lee, *Constitutional Conflicts in Contemporary Malaysia* (1995) ch 3 ('The Judiciary under Siege').

[98] See Albert J Beveridge, *The Life of John Marshall*, above n 38, at chs 1, 2, 3 and 4. The quotation is at 220. See also, Raoul Berger, *Impeachment: The Constitutional Problems* (1973) ch VIII ('The Impeachment of Justice Samuel Chase'). In the course of his tenure as Chief Justice, Earl Warren faced campaigns for his impeachment: see Bernard Schwartz, *Super Chief*, above n 93, at 280–1.

[99] See Henry J Abraham, *Justices, Presidents, and Senators. A History of the US Supreme Court Appointments from Washington to Clinton* (new and revised edn, 1999).

he qualified at the Bar at the age of 55 and brought out in 1868 the first edition of *Benjamin on Sales*. He ended his career as a successful Queen's Counsel.[100] A different figure in the history of the Supreme Court was James Clark McReynolds who served as an Associate Justice from 1914 to 1941: he was so anti-Semitic that he refused to speak to Brandeis for three years after Brandeis's appointment, and he has also been described as loud, cantankerous, sarcastic, aggressive, intemperate and reactionary.[101]

The method of appointment to the federal judiciary in the United States is perhaps unique. Even so the litany of controversies over particular nominations, even in recent decades, provides a fascinating back-drop in considering the independence and stability of judicial systems. Mention could be made of ultimately defeated nominations of Clement F Haynsworth Jr, a 'respected jurist' but eliminated for alleged financial improprieties'[102]; G Harold Carswell, seen as a mediocre lawyer, only for a senator for Nebraska to assert that even,

> if he is mediocre there are a lot of mediocre judges and people and lawyers. They are entitled to a little representation, aren't they, and a little chance?'[103]

and especially of Robert H Bork whose nomination was defeated in 1987 despite his high scholarly and intellectual reputation because of alleged conservative leanings on such matters as abortion and civil rights.[104] Sometimes nominees for the Supreme Court—such as Congressman Richard H Poff in 1971 or Harriet Miers in 2005—have withdrawn from the fray ahead of any Senate proceedings.[105] The appointment of judges in other countries may be less fettered but can nevertheless be highly controversial: consider, for example, Lord Halsbury's appointment in the later 19th century to the High Court bench in England and Wales[106] or, with regard to the High Court as the top federal court in Australia, the appointment in 1975 of Justice Lionel Murphy who had had a 'controversial political career.'[107] Not surprisingly there are regular pressures for reform of the process of appointment,

---

[100] See Justice Ruth Bader Ginsburg, 'From Benjamin to Breyer: Is there a Jewish Seat?' (2003) XXIV *The Supreme Court Historical Society Quarterly* 1 and 4; Martin R Taylor, 'The Amazing Story of Judah P Benjamin, QC', Pt 1, 61 *The Advocate* 657 (2003) and Pt 2, 62 *The Advocate* 823 (2004).

[101] Henry T Abraham, above n 100, at 133.

[102] *Ibid*, at 10–11. See John P Frank, *Clement Haynsworth, the Senate and the Supreme Court* (1991).

[103] Henry T Abraham, above n 100, at 11. See also, John P Frank, above n 103, at ch x.

[104] See Robert H Bork, *The Tempting of America. The Political Seduction of the Law* (1990); Ethan Bronner, *Battle for Justice. How the Bork Nomination Shook America* (1989).

[105] See Henry T Abraham, above n 100, at 14, on the Poff nomination. The Miers nomination was difficult from the start: see George F Will in *The Washington Post*, 5 October 2005, at A23.

[106] See RFV Heuston, *Lives of the Lord Chancellors 1885–1940* (1964) ch v.

[107] See Enid Campbell and HP Lee, above n 57, at 77–9; David Marr, *Barwick* (1980) at 245–7. Some years later, while still on the High Court, Justice Murphy was convicted of attempting to pervert the course of justice and was sentenced to 18 months in jail, but the conviction was quashed on appeal by the New South Wales Court of Appeal: see Campbell and Lee, at 102–3.

and the establishment in England and Wales of the Judicial Appointments Commission under the Constitutional Reform Act reflects such pressures.

Other aspects of judicial independence illustrate the varying laws and practices of different countries. Security of tenure, in direct line from the Act of Settlement, is obviously crucial, and every effort is nowadays made in this country, through the work of the Senior Salaries Review Body—on which I served for six years—to ensure detached advice on the appropriate remuneration for the entire judiciary.[108] There can be striking variations from one jurisdiction to another in the judicial approach to extra-judicial duties such as chairing or conducting inquiries set up by the executive.[109] In the United States a strict view is taken about extra-judicial duties, though at the same time some Supreme Court judges have confidentially advised the executive on highly sensitive matters: Justice Frankfurter was close to President Roosevelt during the Second World War[110] and during the Johnson years Justice Abe Fortes has been described as 'part of the judicial branch and, as well, an unofficial member of the executive branch.'[111] Jurisdictions may vary on the desirability or otherwise of retiring ages, and only this year the issue of 'the lengthening tenure in office of Supreme Court justices' has been extensively analysed in a published symposium.[112]

The variations in and the occasional bitter controversies bound up in efforts to secure independent and stable judicial systems are widely recognised. It is an area where generalisations are perilous, and to no small extent my purpose has been to demonstrate that we are still in a number of jurisdictions seeking to build on the achievements and aspirations of the 17th century. Amid the varied discussions of the appropriate role of the judiciary, of changing methods and standards of judicial accountability, and of ways of securing judicial independence, it is possible to detect a genuine public concern to protect the judiciary from parliamentary or executive encroachment on their spheres of activity. Sir Edward Coke would have been sharply aware of the democratic importance of the debates. For the moment, however, I would like to break off this lecture by echoing, but with great respect, Edward R Murrow's words: 'Good Night, and Good Luck.'

[108] See the various Reports, including the Annual Reports, of the SSRB.

[109] See Enid Campbell and HP Lee, above n 57, at ch 7 ('Extra-Judicial Activities of Judges'); John Griffith, *The Politics of the Judiciary* (5th edn, 1997) Pt 1, ch 2; Sir David Williams, 'Bias: The Judges and the Separation of Powers' [2000] *PL* 45, at 48–55; Alpheus Thomas Mason, 'Extra-Judicial Work for Judges: The View of Chief Justice Stone' (1953) 67 *Harvard Law Review* 193; Diana Woodhouse, 'Judges and the Lord Chancellor', above n 54; J Beatson, 'Should Judges Conduct Public Inquiries' (2005) 121 *LQR* 221.

[110] See Melvin I Urofsky, *Felix Frankfurter. Judicial Restraint and Individual Liberties* (1991) ch 5.

[111] See Laura Kalman, *Abe Fortes. A Biography* (1990) 310, 310–18, 339–40. On the role of Chief Justice Barwick in the Governor-General's decision to dismiss Gough Whitlam in 1975, see David Marr, *Barwick*, above n 108, at ch 19.

[112] Roger C Cramton and Paul D Carrington (eds), *Reforming the Court. Term Limits for Supreme Court Justices* (2006) 3 and generally.

4

The Role of Leadership in the Creation and Maintenance of the Rule of Law

RT HON LORD BINGHAM OF CORNHILL

Delivered at the Hon Society of the Middle Temple on 21st February 2007

THE RULE OF law was not born fully formed when Dicey coined the expression in 1885 in his justly famous book.[1] The concept had roots deep in the past. Some authors, not implausibly, have traced them back to Aristotle's *Politics*[2] where, in a modern translation, he wrote:

> The rule of law, so the argument continues, is preferable to that of an individual; and on the same principle, even if it be better that individuals should govern, they should be appointed only as guardians or ministers of the law ... He, therefore, who would have law rule seems to advocate the exclusive rule of God and Reason; but he who would commit the government to a man adds a brutish element. Appetite is a wild beast, and passion perverts the minds of rulers, even when they are the best of men. Law may thus be defined as 'reason unaffected by passion.'[3]

It will also be recalled that, even in the outlying provinces of the Roman Empire, St Paul's status as a Roman citizen enabled him to protest at being punished before he had been tried,[4] and entitled him to appeal to Caesar:

> Then said Paul, I stand at Caesar's judgment seat, where I ought to be judged ... I appeal unto Caesar. Then Festus, when he had conferred with the council, answered, Hast thou appealed unto Caesar? unto Caesar shalt thou go.[5]

Thus one may perhaps see Caesar as the distant precursor of the Judicial Committee of the Privy Council.

---

[1] *An Introduction to the Study of the Law of the Constitution* (London, 1885).
[2] Brian Tamanaha, *On the Rule of Law* (Cambridge, 2004) 8–9.
[3] See *Aristotle's Politics and Athenian Constitution* (edited and translated by John Warrington) (JM Dent 1959) Book 111, s 1287, p 97. More literally translated, the passage opens: 'It is better for the law to rule than one of the citizens' and continues: 'so even the guardians of the laws are obeying the laws.'
[4] Acts of the Apostles 16:22–40; 22:24–30.
[5] *Ibid*, 25:10–12.

Let me hasten to say that I shall not attempt to trace the intellectual and historical roots of the rule of law, a task which, if comprehensively undertaken, would overrun the 400th anniversary of the founding of Jamestown and last almost until the 400th anniversary of the Second Charter of Virginia. Instead, rather self-indulgently perhaps, I shall focus on eight events, of varied historical significance no doubt, but all of them in my opinion recognisable as staging posts on the journey to the rule of law as we know it today. Having touched on each event, I shall seek where possible to identify the individual or individuals who can, more than others, claim credit for a leadership role. My account will, I fear, be episodic, impressionistic, superficial and idiosyncratic: others might trace a different route to the same destination. Having in this dilettante manner addressed the role of leadership in the creation of the rule of law, I shall touch, very much more briefly, on the role of leadership in its maintenance.

My point of embarkation is Magna Carta 1215. Even in translation, the terms of chapters 39 and 40 have the power to make the blood race:

> 39. No free man shall be seized or imprisoned, or stripped of his rights or possessions, or outlawed or exiled, or deprived of his standing in any other way, nor will we proceed with force against him, or send others to do so, except by the lawful judgment of his equals or by the law of the land.
>
> 40. To no one will we sell, to no one deny or delay right or justice.

These are words that should be printed on the stationery of the Department of Constitutional Affairs and the Home Office in place of the rather vapid slogans that their letters now carry.

The contemporary significance of Magna Carta has of course been misrepresented and exaggerated. It did not embody the principles of jury trial, which was still in its infancy, or habeas corpus, which in its modern form had yet to be invented[6]. The language of chapter 39 has been criticised as 'vague and unsatisfactory'[7] and it has been said that chapter 40 'has had much read into it that would have astonished its framers.'[8] But, with all allowances made, Magna Carta was an event that changed the constitutional landscape in this country and, over time, the world.

The Charter deserves to be remembered for two reasons above all. First, and in contrast with other European charters of the period, including the Golden Bull of Hungary of 1222, it was a grant to all free men throughout the realm.[9] It assumed legal parity among all free men to an exceptional degree, contributing to a sense of community that may, perhaps, help to explain our happy freedom from bloody revolution. Secondly, it represented

[6] Sir W Holdsworth, *A History of English Law* (4th edn, Methuen/Sweet & Maxwell 1936) vol 11, 215.

[7] JC Holt, *Magna Carta and Medieval Government* (Hambledon Press 1985) 196.

[8] WS McKechnie, *Magna Carta* (2nd edn, Glasgow, James Maclehose 1914) 395.

[9] JC Holt., *Magna Carta* (Cambridge, 1992) 276–8.

and expressed a clear rejection of unbridled royal power, an assertion that even the supreme power in the state must be subject to certain overriding rules. Here, clearly recognisable, is the embryo of the rule of law.

In school textbooks on the period, there was, I think, a tendency to portray Magna Carta as a response to the tyrannous oppression and exactions of King John. Such an interpretation was no doubt easy to teach, and one need not doubt that hostility to the firm government of King John, exacerbated by his dispute with the church, acted as a catalyst. But the terms of Magna Carta drew heavily on earlier models, not least King Henry I's charter of liberties and the coronation oaths of previous kings. The coronation oath included a promise to exercise justice and mercy in all judgments, an oath still (with minor modification) prescribed by section 3 of the Coronation Oath Act 1688 and sworn by the Queen in 1953. In the erudite judgment of Dr McKechnie:

> Looking both to the contents and the formalities of execution of John's Great Charter, the safer opinion would seem to be, that, like the English Constitution, it is of mixed origin, deriving elements from ancestors of more races than one; but that the traditional line of descent from the oaths and writs of Anglo-Saxon kings, through the Charter of Henry I, is one that cannot be neglected.[10]

It is similarly unhistorical to see Magna Carta as a sudden response to a short-term problem. As the greatest modern authority on the charter, Sir James Holt, has written:

> Magna Carta was not a sudden intrusion into English society and politics. On the contrary, it grew out of them. There is no need to deny the influence of Langton, other churchmen, or the king's officials and clerks. There is equally no need to suggest that they simply conjured all that was best in Magna Carta out of their intellects and their canonical or theological training. The evidence will not stand this construction. Nor yet does it support the case that the Charter stood for something outside the scope of lay thinking and above the mundane interest and ambitions of the temporal world. It is a mistake to couch the argument in terms of selfishness or altruism. Laymen had been assuming, discussing and applying the principles of Magna Carta long before 1215. They could grasp it well enough. But they were not for that reason unselfish. The barons did not talk of free men out of loftiness of purpose, or make concessions to knights and burgesses out of generosity. They did so because the political situation required it and because the structure of English society and government allowed them to do no other.[11]

Who, then, designed Magna Carta? This is a question which Sir James Holt also poses. But his answer, unsurprising from so learned a source, would not be suitable for a television quiz game:

> In answering this, historians have differed markedly. While Stubbs considered that the baronage were at least partly responsible, and Tout wrote of Robert FitzWalter

---

[10] *Ibid*, 94–5.
[11] JC Holt, *Magna Carta* 395.

as 'the first champion of English liberty', Miss Norgate firmly asserted that the barons were incapable of rising to the 'lofty conception embodied in the Charter' and that Stephen Langton and the bishops were its chief authors. Some later authorities have restated her views, in whole or in part, while recently Dr Lane Poole has looked to King John's friends and supporters, rather than the rebel leaders, for evidence of political experience and sagacity. Sir Maurice Powicke, in contrast, has argued that, as important administrators, justices and associates of lawyers and clerks, the barons were bound to absorb and hold views on the organization of the state.[12]

So Magna Carta was not the achievement of any single person. But although Stephen Langton's share in the struggle for the charter is not, as one great authority has said, 'free from perplexity',[13] it is perhaps he more than anyone who deserves credit for masterminding the outcome. In Holt's judgment, Langton was not responsible for all that was best in the charter, but he was very influential, not as an originator but as a mediator moderator.[14] He was concerned that kings should act according to law and after proper judgment, and his was probably the mind responsible for the attempt to set down in writing what the barons wanted and to frame it in a way which would bind the King.[15] He helped to create the climate in which Magna Carta could be produced.

My first staging post en route to the rule of law is the writ of habeas corpus ad subjiciendum.[16] The issue of a writ to secure the presence in court of a defendant or criminal suspect was familiar by the early 13th century, but it was not at that stage used to protect the liberty of the subject or investigate the lawfulness of a person's detention. That came later, when the writ was issued with a writ seeking an order of certiorari, and its development owed much to the jurisdictional struggle between the common law courts and the Court of Chancery and the Court of High Commission.[17] The substantive remedy of habeas corpus was not, as already observed, a product of Magna Carta, but came over time, however unhistorically, to be seen as such. Thus one can accept the truth of Sir William Holdsworth's judgment concerning the protection of personal liberty in this country:

> Without the inspiration of a general principle with all the prestige of Magna Carta behind it, this development could never have taken place; and, equally, without the translation of that principle into practice, by the invention of specific writs to deal with cases of its infringement, it could never have taken practical shape.[18]

---

[12] *Magna Carta and Medieval Government*, n 7 above, 179–80.
[13] FM Powicke, *Stephen Langton* (Oxford, 1928) 129.
[14] *Magna Carta*, n 8 above, 281.
[15] Christopher Holdsworth, *Oxford Dictionary of National Biography* (Oxford, OUP 2004), Stephen Langton.
[16] I base my summary on the helpful account of RJ Sharpe, *The Law of Habeas Corpus* (2nd edn, Oxford, 1989) 1–8.
[17] Sir W Holdsworth, n 6 above, vol IX, 104–14.
[18] *Ibid*, vol IX, 104.

The writ of habeas corpus ad subjiciendum emerged as an effective means of affording protection against unlawful detention, perhaps the most effective protection against executive lawlessness ever devised. In *Bushell's Case* in 1670, Vaughan CJ was able to assert as simple fact:

> The writ of habeas corpus is now the most usual remedy by which a man is restored again to his liberty, if he have been against law deprived of it.[19]

But this is a tale without named heroes. The historical record does not, to my knowledge, identify any practitioner or any judge as the 'onlie begetter' or inspiration of this important remedy. It was more probably the result of those 'little, nameless, unremembered acts' that usually comprise organic development of the law. But perhaps room may be found for one, probably apocryphal, hero. One of the charges in the impeachment of Clarendon in 1668 was that he had caused 'divers of his majesty's subjects to be imprisoned against law, in remote islands, garrisons and other places' where the writ of habeas corpus did not run 'thereby to prevent them from the benefit of the law'[20]—an ingenious idea, not unknown in more recent times. Legislative measures to remedy this obvious abuse were adopted by the House of Commons on five occasions during the 1670s, but foundered in the Lords until, in 1679, a further comprehensive Habeas Corpus Amendment Act achieved a majority in that House also. But the majority in the Lords was 57 to 55 and, if Bishop Burnet is to be believed, even that majority was only achieved because Lord Grey, acting as teller for the ayes, succeeded, without his opposite number noticing, in counting a very fat Lord as 10.[21]

My next staging post, the Petition of Right 1628, is a lineal descendant of Magna Carta and habeas corpus and is perhaps as important a contributor to the rule of law as either. Its genesis has been the subject in recent years of acute scholarly controversy,[22] and much of the detailed history is debatable. But the broad picture is reasonably clear. Moved by hostility to the Duke of Buckingham, the House of Commons in 1625 and 1626 denied Charles I the means to conduct military operations abroad that Buckingham was to command. The King was unwilling to give up his military ambitions and resorted to the expedient of a forced loan to finance it. A number of those subject to this imposition declined to pay, and some were imprisoned, among them the Five Knights: Sir Thomas Darnel, Sir John Corbel, Sir Walter Erie, Sir John Heveningham and Sir Edmund Hampden. Each

---

[19] *Bushell's Case* (1670) Vaughan 135 at 136.
[20] *Clarendon* (1668) 6 St Tr 291 at 330, 396.
[21] *Burnet, History of My Own Times*, vol (i), 485.
[22] See JA Guy, 'The Origins of the Petition of Right Reconsidered' (1982) *Historical Journal* 289–312; MB Young, 'The Origins of the Petition of Right Reconsidered Further' (1984) *Historical Journal* 449–52; Mark Kishlansky, 'Tyranny Denied: Charles 1, Attorney General Heath, and the Five Knights' Case' (1999) *Historical Journal* 53–83.

of them sought a writ of habeas corpus to secure his release. Sir Thomas Darnel was rebuffed at an early stage and gave up the fight. The other four fought on, each represented by eminent counsel, who included John Selden. Their hope was that non-payment of the loan would be given as the reason for their imprisonment, whereupon the lawfulness of the loan could be challenged and investigated in court. But the Crown frustrated this hope by stating that the initial commitment and continued detention of the knights was 'per speciale mandatum domini regis', by his majesty's special commandment. Four King's Bench judges, headed by the Chief Justice, before whom the matter came, had no knowledge, judicially, of why the knights were in prison, and made a simple order (with no final judgment) remanding the knights back to prison.

This proceeding was not as novel, nor perhaps as shocking, as the subsequent furore might lead one to infer. The judges' order was, it seems, an interlocutory refusal of bail and followed a familiar form. Those detained were released once the collection of the loan was complete, shortly after the hearing, and this may always have been the intention. Detention at the instance of the executive without charge or trial was not without precedent at the time, But the Commons, when they assembled in 1628, had no appetite for points like these. It was, as Conrad Russell has written, 'a one-issue Parliament.'[23] It had 'the conscious and deliberate aim of vindicating English liberties.'[24] The outcome of the *Five Knights' Case* was one of the issues that fired this determination, Allied with it were the expropriation of personal property, by means of a forced loan, without parliamentary sanction; the billeting of soldiers; and resort to martial law. The parliamentary leadership—a formidable body including Sir Edward Coke, Sir John Eliot, John Pym, John Selden, Edward Littleton, Sir Nathaniel Rich, Sir Robert Phelips, Sir Dudley Digges, Sir John Glanville and others—saw the action of the Crown in these areas as a threat to that ideal of liberty that they claimed as a birthright. And the disquiet to which the decision in the *Five Knights Case* gave rise is not hard to understand: for even if it was no more than an interlocutory decision on bail, the question inevitably arose whether the power of the King to detain without charge or trial was subject to any legal constraint, and if so what.

As is normal in such situations, both sides claimed to be defending the status quo. The leaders of the Commons invoked Magna Carta and later precedents, disavowing reliance on any novel principle. The King for his part declared his loyalty to old laws and customs, while resisting any surrender of his existing prerogative. But in truth the Commons were seeking to establish, more clearly and comprehensively than ever before, the

[23] *Parliaments and English Politics 1621–1629* (Oxford, 1979) 344.
[24] *Ibid*, 343.

supremacy of the law. On 26 April 1628, Sir Thomas Wentworth, a moderate influence in the Commons, expressed the hope that

> it shall never be stirred here whether the King be above the law or the law be above the King.[25]

But that was the very issue the majority wanted to resolve, in favour of the law. They had not only political reasons for seeking that outcome but also, with many common lawyers prominent among them, professional reasons also. For if one of the ingredients of these debates was distrust of the King, another was doubt about the capacity of the common law to protect the subject. 'If this be law', asked Sir Robert Phelips on 22 March 1628, 'what do we talk of our liberties?'[26] The leadership chose to restore trust in the law, and that precluded any workable settlement with the King.[27]

Thus it was that the Petition of Right came to be accepted by a reluctant Lords and eventually, on 7 June 1628, an even more reluctant King, who shortly thereafter sought to qualify his unqualified assent. Remarkably, although only in form a petition, this instrument was treated and printed as a statute.[28] Having invoked Magna Carta and the reference to due process in the reissued charter of 1354, clause V provided:

> Nevertheless against the tenor of the said statutes and other the good laws and statutes of your realm to that end provided, divers of your subjects have of late been imprisoned without any cause shown; and when for their deliverance they were brought before your justices by your Majesty's writ of habeas corpus there to undergo and receive as the Court should order, and their Keepers commanded to certify the causes of their detainer, no cause was certified, but that they were detained by your Majesty's special command signified by the lords of your Privy Council, and yet were returned back to several prisons without being charged with any thing to which they might make answer according to the law.[29]

And the conclusion came in clause VIII:

> They do therefore humbly pray your most excellent majesty that no, man hereafter be compelled to make or yield any gift, loan, benevolence, tax or such like charge without common consent by act of parliament, and that none be called to make answer or take such oath or to give attendance or be confined or otherwise molested or disquieted concerning the same or for refusal thereof. And that no

---

[25] See Robert C Johnson and others (eds), *Commons Debates 1628* (Yale Center for Parliamentary History 1977) vol III, 98.

[26] *Ibid,* vol II, 63.

[27] Russell, *op cit.,* p 350.

[28] Elizabeth Read Foster, 'Printing the Petition of Right' *Huntington Library Quarterly*, vol XXXVIII No 1 (November 1974) 81–2.

[29] The text of the Petition is found in many places, conveniently in JP Kenyon, *The Stuart Constitution 1603–1688* (2nd edn, Cambridge, 1986) 68.

freeman in any such manner as is before mentioned be imprisoned or detained. And that your Majesty would be pleased to remove the said soldiers and mariners, and that your people may not be so burdened in time to come. And that the aforesaid commissions for proceeding by martial law may be revoked and annulled. And that hereafter no commissions of like nature may issue forth to any person or persons whatsoever to be executed as aforesaid, lest by colour of them any of your Majesty's subjects be destroyed or put to death contrary to the laws and franchises of the land.

If there is one moment when the rule of law may be said to have come of age, the acceptance of the Petition of Right, for me, is it.

My next staging post is a good deal less obvious. But if, as I think, the rule of law depends on the existence of judges conscientiously seeking to act judicially—without fear or favour, affection or ill-will, independently and impartially—it is worth pausing to mention Sir Mathew Hale, Chief Justice of the King's Bench from 1671–76. Hale is not the only judge to have reminded himself in writing what judicial conduct requires. The late Lord Ackner, at first instance, propped up on the bench in front of him a card on which he had written 'You are paid to listen.' But Hale's 'Things Necessary to be Continually had in Remembrance', dating from the 1660s and for his own guidance, is the best early statement known to me of rules to govern judicial conduct. He enjoined himself, among other things:

> 4 That in the execution of justice, I carefully lay aside my own passions, and not give way to them however provoked.
>
> 6 That I suffer not myself to be prepossessed with any judgment at all, till the whole business and both parties be heard.
>
> 7 That I never engage myself in the beginning of any cause, but reserve myself unprejudiced till the whole be heard.
>
> 11 That popular or court applause or distaste, have no influence into any thing I do in point of justice.
>
> 12. Not to be solicitous what men will say or think, so long as I keep myself according to the rule of justice.
>
> 16. To abhor all private solicitations of whatever kind soever and by whomsoever in matters depending.

But there may, I suppose, even today, be judges who neglect his last injunction:

> 18 To be short and sparing at meals that I may be fitter for business.

The Bill of Rights 1689 and the Act of Settlement 1701 both sealed and extended the achievements of the Petition of Right and the Long Parliament. No monarch could again rely on divine authority to override the law.[30] The

---

[30] Holdsworth, n 6 above, vol VI, 230.

authority and independence of Parliament were proclaimed[31]; the integrity of its proceedings was protected[32] and there could be no standing army in time of peace without its sanction.[33] The power to suspend laws without the consent of Parliament was condemned as illegal.[34] So was the power of dispensing with laws or the execution of laws 'as it hath been assumed and exercised of late'[35]—a provision that it was intended to clarify by further legislation,[36] but which never eventuated.[37] Personal liberty and security were protected by prohibiting the requirement of excessive fines,[38] the imposition of excessive bail[39] and the infliction of cruel and unusual punishments.[40] Jury trial was protected.[41] In addition, the tenure of office of the high judiciary was secured upon its present basis.[42] Coupled with the very much older rule which rendered the higher judiciary immune from civil suit or criminal prosecution for acts done in a judicial capacity,[43] the foundation of judicial independence was securely laid.

The architects of the Bill of Rights and the Act of Settlement must be recognised as leaders in the creation of the rule of law. Who were they? Credit for the Bill of Rights must, I think, go to the committee of 35 members appointed by what passed for the House of Commons who, in the first fortnight of February 1689, drew up the declaration which, after amendment by Lords and Commons, was formally accepted by the Prince and Princess of Orange, as a condition of their acceding to the throne, in the Banqueting House in Whitehall on Wednesday 13 February.[44] The declaration, with minor amendments, was in due course enacted and received the royal assent on 16 December 1689.[45] But the bargain—a constitutional compact—had already been struck: the Crown had been offered and accepted on terms. The first draft of the Bill of Rights had included a provision safeguarding the tenure of the judges and protection of their salaries,[46] but this was dropped when it was decided (in the face of resistance by the Prince) that the Bill should confirm old rights and not create new ones.[47]

---

[31] Bill of Rights, I.4, 8.
[32] *Ibid*, I.9.
[33] *Ibid*, I.1.
[34] *Ibid*, I.1.
[35] *Ibid*, 1.2.
[36] *Ibid*, XII.
[37] Holdsworth, n 6 above, vol VI, 240.
[38] Bill of Rights, I.10.
[39] *Ibid.*
[40] *Ibid.*
[41] *Ibid*, I.11.
[42] Act of Settlement, s 3.
[43] Holdsworth, n 6 above, vol VI, pp 234–40.
[44] David Lewis Jones, *A Parliamentary History of the Glorious Revolution* (HMSO), Introduction, 24–46.
[45] *Ibid*, 49.
[46] *Ibid*, 29.
[47] *Ibid*, 38–40.

When in 1701 Parliament came to provide for the protestant succession to Anne, the opportunity was taken to enact the same provision. The measure was guided through the Commons by Robert Harley, later the first earl of Oxford, then MP for New Radnor and Speaker.[48] There was no division in either House.[49] For another 60 years judicial tenure remained problematical (on the accession of a new monarch a judge need not be re-appointed, and some were not)[50] but it was a crucial step on the way to judicial independence.

The Constitution of the United States of course marked another crucial staging-post in the history of the rule of law. It was not the first attempt to draft a document laying down the respective powers and duties of the different institutions of government. Oliver Cromwell's Instrument of Government of 1653, and perhaps other models, anticipated it. But the US Constitution was ground-breaking in its enlightened attempt to create a strong and effective central government while at the same time preserving the autonomy of the individual states and (in the first 10 Amendments) protecting the fundamental rights of the individual against what one contemporary commentator called 'the form of elective despotism.'[51] It was also ground-breaking in being the product not of the diktat of a ruling clique but of wide-ranging, very high quality debate,[52] and genuine democratic endorsement. But the single most revolutionary feature of the Constitution was, I think to be found in Article VI:

> This Constitution, and the Laws of the United States which shall be made in pursuance thereof; and all Treaties made, or which shall be made, under the Authority of the United States, shall be the supreme Law of the Land; and the Judges in every State shall be bound thereby, any Thing in the Constitution or Laws of any State to the Contrary notwithstanding.

Thus the Congress (Article 1), the President (Article II) and the federal judiciary (Article III) were to have such powers as were conferred by or under the Constitution, and none other. This contrasted, and continues to contrast, with the legislative omnipotence theoretically enjoyed by the Crown in Parliament. The point was clearly made by 'A Freeman' to the

---

[48] WA Speck, 'Harley, Robert, first earl of Oxford and Mortimer (1661–1724)', *Oxford Dictionary of National Biography* (Oxford, OUP 2004).

[49] Robert Stevens, 'The Act of Settlement and the Questionable History of Judicial Independence' (2001) *Oxford University Commonwealth Law Journal* 259.

[50] *Ibid*, 262.

[51] Richard Henry Lee in a letter to Samuel Adams, 5 October 1787: see Richard Lubinski, *James Madison and the Struggle for the Bill of Rights* (Oxford, 2006) 40. Whether Lord Hailsham had this reference in mind, consciously or unconsciously when, in his Dimbleby Lecture of 1976 he made his much-misquoted reference to 'elective dictatorship' can only, I think, be a matter for conjecture.

[52] See, for example, Bernard Bailyn (ed), *The Debate on the Constitution* (The Library of America 1993) Parts One and Two.

Freeholders and Freemen of Rhode Island on 20 March 1788. Of the British Parliament he correctly said:

> They are the supreme Legislative, their powers are absolute, and extend to an abolition of Magna Carta itself.

The Congress was different:

> Their powers are not supreme, nor absolute, it being defined by the Constitution: and all powers therein not granted, are retained by the State Legislatures.[53]

So, for the first time, I think, the law as expressed in the Constitution was to be supreme, binding not only the executive and the judges but also the legislature itself. This was indeed an advance for the rule of law, giving the law of the Constitution, as interpreted by the Supreme Court, an authority it had never before enjoyed anywhere. The architects of this dispensation, who laboured mightily to achieve it, are justly celebrated, with James Madison, Alexander Hamilton, John Jay, Gouverneur Morris, Rufus King, James Wilson, Edmund Randolph—and, of course, the President, George Washington—heading the list.[54]

I turn to a development of a rather different character, one occurring not at a particular time but taking effect over centuries, although with increasing momentum over the last century or so. I refer to the attempt to establish legally recognised standards of state conduct, even in relation to the use of force (the *ius ad bellum*, now governed by the United Nations Charter) and the conduct of war or armed conflict (the *ius in bella*), Rules to restrain the brutality inherent in war were familiar in classical times[55] and during the Middle Ages.[56] Under the influence of writers such as Gentili[57] and Grotius[58] a body of customary international law began to grow up, fed by sources such as the 150 Articles of War signed by King Gustavus Adolpus II of Sweden in 1621. On occasion such rules were the subject of bilateral treaty, as in the 1785 Treaty between the United States and Prussia which, although one of Amity and Commerce, contained provisions to be applied if war between them were to occur. Thus Article 23 defined the immunity

---

[53] *Ibid*, Part Two, 369.

[54] Max Farrand, *The Fathers of the Constitution* (Yale, 1921).

[55] Coleman Phillipson, *The International Law and Custom of Ancient Greece and Rome* (Macmillan 1911) vol II, 166–384.

[56] Maurice Keen, *The Laws of War in the Late Middle Ages* (London, Routledge and Kegal Paul 1965). Both Richard II in 1385 and Henry V during the Agincourt campaign in 1415 issued ordinances to govern the conduct of their soldiers vis-à-vis the enemy: see Juliet Barker, *Agincourt* (Abacus 2006) 169, 223.

[57] He was Regius Professor of Civil Law at Oxford when he published his most important work, *De Jure Belli* (1625).

[58] *De Jure Belli et Pacis* (1625).

of merchants, women, children, scholars, cultivators and others. Article 24 provided for proper treatment of prisoners of war, and began:

> And to prevent the destruction of prisoners of war by sending them into distant and inclement countries, or by crowding them into close and noxious places, the two contracting parties solemnly pledge themselves to each other and to the world that they will not adopt any such practice.[59]

Over the last century and a half, decisions of international courts and tribunals and the opinions of the learned have been influential in setting the standards of permissible conduct in war, but the scene has been dominated by a plethora of international conventions addressing different aspects of this multi-faceted subject. The history of these conventions yields a rich and diverse gallery of heroes, from whom any selection is to some extent invidious. But certain figures stand out. Among them is that of Jean Henry Dunant, whose book *A Memory of Solferino*,[60] published in 1862, describing the horrific aftermath of the battle that he had witnessed, inspired the first, 1864, Geneva Convention on the Treatment of the Wounded[61] and the foundation of the International Committee of the Red Cross. Also worthy of mention is the Tsar Alexander II, who convened the conference which promulgated the 1868 St Petersburg Declaration Renouncing the Use, in Time of War, of Explosive Projectiles under 400 Grammes Weight, a declaration to which 19 states assented.[62] The initiative of Alexander II was taken further by his grandson, Tsar Nicholas II, who convened the First Hague Peace Conference in 1899, which led to three conventions and three declarations. One of the declarations, to which Great Britain acceded despite initial objections, related to a type of bullet first manufactured at the British Indian arsenal of Dum-Dum, near Calcutta.[63] The Second Hague Peace Conference of 1907, convened at the instance first of President Theodore Roosevelt and then of Tsar Nicholas II also, was even more productive, giving rise to 13 conventions and one declaration, most of them directed to the conduct of war on land and sea.[64] Among many conventions made after the Second World War under the auspices of the United Nations, special mention may perhaps be made of the 1948 United Nations Convention on the Prevention and Punishment of the Crime of Genocide, the eventual outcome of a request made to the Secretary-General by the delegations of Cuba, India and Panama.[65] In this much-abbreviated roll of honour I would also include Gustave Moynier,

---

[59] See Adam Roberts and Richard Guelff (eds), *Documents on the Laws of War* (3rd edn, Oxford, 2000) 4.

[60] Republished by the International Committee of the Red Cross (Geneva, 1986).

[61] This Convention was superseded by the first of the four 1949 Geneva Conventions, a greatly expanded version of the 10-article original.

[62] See Roberts and Guelff, n 59 above, 53–7.

[63] *Ibid*, 63–6.

[64] *Ibid*, 67–137.

[65] *Ibid*, 179–94.

one of the founders of the International Committee of the Red Cross, who in 1872 urged the establishment of an international criminal court to adjudicate on violations of the 1864 Geneva Convention on Treatment of the Wounded. His wish was fulfilled on ratification of the 1998 Rome Statute of the International Criminal Court, although one has to record with regret the opposition of the United States, a strong supporter of the proposal in its earlier stages and a strong supporter of International Criminal Tribunals established for the former Yugoslavia and Rwanda in 1993 and 1994.[66] It is easy to disparage all these rules as ineffective and difficult to enforce. Many have done so. But to the extent that they have led to anyone—combatants, wounded, prisoners of war, women, children, civilians, non-combatants—being spared the full horror of unrestrained warfare, they must be accounted a victory for the rule of law.

My final port of call (to vary the metaphor) is the Universal Declaration of Human Rights, adopted by the General Assembly of the United Nations in Paris on 10 December 1948 with 48 votes in favour, 8 abstentions[67] and no votes against. Contrary to the original wishes of the British and of Rene Cassin,[68] the influential French delegate and negotiator, the declaration is not of course binding. But, drawing on Magna Carta, the Bill of Rights 1689, the French Declaration of the Rights of Man and the Citizen of 1789 and the American Bill of Rights of 1791, it has provided the common standard for human rights upon which formal treaty commitments have subsequently been founded and has inspired the International Covenant on Civil and Political Rights 1966, the International Covenant on Economic, Social and Cultural Rights 1966, the International Covenant on the Elimination of All Forms of Racial Discrimination 1966 and regional treaties such as the European Convention on Human Rights 1950, the American Convention on Human Rights 1969, the African Charter on Human and Peoples' Rights 1981 and the Arab Convention on Human Rights 1991.[69]

The framers of the Universal Declaration sought, or received, advice from many sources, which included the Huxleys (Julian and Aldous), HG Wells, Teilhard de Chardin and Benedetto Croce.[70] The paternity of the Declaration has been the subject of some controversy, and the contribution of René Cassin, though great, has perhaps been exaggerated.[71] In the judgment of John Humphrey, the distinguished Canadian international lawyer who prepared the first draft, the Declaration 'had no father' because

---

[66] *Ibid*, 565–72, 615–21, 667–97.

[67] Byelorussia, Czechoslovakia, Poland, Ukraine, USSR, Yugoslavia, South Africa, Saudi Arabia.

[68] Mary Ann Glendon, *A World Made New* (Random House 2001) 58; Gérard Israël, *René Cassin* (Deselée de Brouwer 1990) 204.

[69] Gillian D Triggs, *International Law: Contemporary Principles and Practices* (Butterworths 2006) 884–5.

[70] Glendon, n 68 above, 51, 56.

[71] Glendon, n 68 above, 65.

'literally hundreds of people ... contributed to its drafting.'[72] But the Declaration was, as Pope John XXIII was to say in his 1963 encyclical *Pacem in Terris*, 'an act of the highest importance' and the role of leadership was exercised by four people in particular: Mrs Eleanor Roosevelt, René Cassin, Charles Malik of Lebanon and PC Chang of China. If, as I think, the rule of law demands protection of fundamental, human rights, these four, more than any others, deserve credit for the almost worldwide acceptance of that principle.

By steps such as these the rule of law has over the centuries been painfully and of course imperfectly established. On whom does its maintenance depend? To whom do we look for leadership in that important task? I give three brief answers.

First, we look to those who have the responsibility for educating and forming public opinion. I lay stress on 'educating', because the rule of law will be the first victim of every national crisis and emergency unless the people at large understand at least in broad outline what it means and believe that it really matters. As it is, every poll of public opinion shows a disturbing willingness to compromise hard-won rights in order to address problems or difficulties that may well be exaggerated or transient. The history of this and other leading Western democracies does not, I suggest, show that unwavering allegiance to the rule of law that one might have expected centuries of tradition to instil.[73] Thus the Director of the Serious Fraud Office could recently speak of balancing 'the need to maintain the rule of law against the wider public interest,'[74] as if adherence to the rule of law were a dispensable *desideratum* and not a foundation of our society. If it is true that the rule of law lacks the deep and instinctive support which, at least in my view, it should attract, it is a reproach to all who in any capacity, as teachers or publicists of any kind, have the opportunity to explore and explain the issues at stake.

For leadership in maintaining the rule of law we must look, secondly, to Parliament. There should, and no doubt usually is, a strong consensus among members of both Houses supportive of the rule of law. But we must on occasion look to those courageous and independent-minded members who have been willing, when they believed that fundamental principles were at stake, to defy the dictates of party allegiance and tabloid clamour. It is to the House of Commons above all that we must look, as we have looked successfully in the past, for the protection of our fundamental rights and liberties.

---

[72] Glendon, n 68 above, 47. Interestingly, both Humphrey and Cassin wanted to include a statement of duties in the Declaration: n 68 above, 76.

[73] See Tom Bingham, 'Personal Freedom and the Dilemma of Democracies' (2003) 52 *ICLQ* 841–58.

[74] Statement quoted by the Attorney-General in the House of Lords: HL, Hansard 14 December 2006, cols 1711–12.

Thirdly, I point to the courts. If, as I think, the rule of law is more than a rhetorical aspiration and is something capable in some contexts at least of legal expression, then the courts must where appropriate give it expression. But the courts are not free agents. Their duty to apply the law imports a duty not to apply what is not the law. They have no mandate, no authority, to do so. But their duty to apply the law according to the best of their judgment, no matter how unwelcome in some quarters their judgment may be, can serve to maintain the rule of law and even, perhaps, promote public understanding of what it entails.

It all seems a long way from Jamestown. But the first Virginia Charter of 10 April 1606 contained a royal declaration,

> that all every the Persons, being our Subjects, which shall dwell and inhabit within every and any of the said several Colonies and Plantations, and every of their children, which shall happen to be born within any of the Limits and Precincts of the said several Colonies and Plantations, shall HAVE and enjoy all Liberties, Franchises and Immunities, within any of our other Dominions, to all Intents and Purposes, as if they had been abiding and born, within this our Realm of England, or any other of our said Dominions ...

So perhaps Jamestown may have seen not only the first permanent British settlement on American soil, and the first Anglican church, and the first representative assembly, but also the first sowing, in what proved to be fertile soil, of what grew into the rule of law.[75]

[75] I have been greatly assisted in preparing this lecture by Matthew Slater, my judicial assistant, and also Diana Procter, to both of whom I am indebted.

5

Raleigh's Legacy

MR JUSTICE COLMAN

Delivered at the Renaissance Centre, Richmond on 13 April 2007

IT IS AS always a great honour and pleasure to be invited to take part in the annual meeting of COMBAR's North America Committee.

It is a particular pleasure to find here today David Steel, who was the first Chairman of COMBAR immediately before I took over, as well as Bill Blair—a very early committee member and later Chairman. It is also a great pleasure to see two of the original members of the North American Liaison Committee that I suggested should be formed at a meeting on 13 November 1989. Those two are our loyal supporters—John McDougall from Toronto and Steve Rosenfeld from New York. It is wonderfully rewarding to see how strong the North American membership has now become. It has grown in strength with COMBAR itself. The latter now has some 1,100 members.

But today I am not going to dwell on the origins of COMBAR in North America but rather on the origins of the British in Virginia. I want to talk in particular about the one man whose obsessive drive and determination led directly to the Jamestown Declaration—Sir Walter Raleigh. And, as this meeting runs parallel to that of the American Inns of Court on the rule of law, I want to dwell on the supreme irony that it was Raleigh who was brought to his end by what we here would now regard as a total travesty of the rule of law.

As I shall explain later, it is quite a coincidence that makes it possible for me to tell you what follows.

By 1584 Raleigh had become Queen Elizabeth's favourite. She in her late forties had grown quite passionate about him, who was about 30, and she bestowed great wealth on him, as well as the monopoly for the exploration and plantation by way of settlement of the southern part of North America. He was determined to establish a settlement there but equally determined to plan this operation with extreme care and on the basis of exhaustive scientific research. Elizabeth had given him a lease of Durham House, an old building of Norman origin, which stood where Embankment Gardens now are, alongside the River Thames, just east of Embankment underground station. There he set up a planning headquarters covering navigation and North American geography, including climate and vegetation. He appointed as advisers the brilliant Oxford mathematician, Harriott and the navigational expert, Hakluyt. In 1584 he sent a reconnaissance expedition which located Roanoke as a suitable site for a settlement. This was an island located within the Outer Banks, not far from where Jamestown was eventually to be founded. The expedition returned to England with two Indians who were duly installed at Durham House so as to enable the local Indian language, Algonkian, to be studied and phoneticised.

Elizabeth refused to put up any money for the settlement. She did however provide one of her own ships, *The Tiger*, together with £400 worth of gunpowder, and she contributed her own very special idea, namely the title for the whole territory which, after all, was to belong to her eventually and was to be Virginia. She appointed Raleigh as controller of the enterprise and knighted him at the beginning of 1585. The expedition to Virginia was planned as the biggest settlement expedition ever undertaken from England. It was financed by the City of London merchants who bought shares in the product of one summer season's privateering against such Spanish vessels as the fleet could capture without going off route!

The destination was to be Roanoke. This small island just south of the eventual site of Jamestown was a hopeless location. It was already over-crowded with Indians and had very little land which was cultivatable, as well as being plagued with mosquitoes.

The expedition was something of a disaster. *The Tiger*, on which practically all the perishable supplies had been loaded, ran aground not far from Roanoke and punctured her hull. Much of the supplies, including vital foodstuffs, animals and grain seed were lost. After the settlers eventually landed, it was realised they did not have enough supplies to support all the settlers through the on-coming winter. In the result only 107 were left at Roanoke and the rest were taken back to England. As it happened, there was not enough food even to support those who remained and there were too many gentry in the party who were neither willing nor able to hunt or fish or cultivate the land. Worse still, as the food situation and the general conditions deteriorated, they all fell out with each other.

After a very, very hard winter, during which the settlers were dependent on buying what little food they could get from the Indians, Raleigh had sent out a relieving party with further supplies. However, Sir Francis Drake, who was on his way back from having sacked the Spanish settlement at Santo Domingo in Hispaniola, arrived at Roanoke with a fleet of some 23 ships, rescued most of the surviving settlers and took them home. Among them was Harriott, who brought back samples of wild tobacco from Roanoke and he and Raleigh then promoted the use of tobacco at court, ostensibly for medicinal purposes, and so initiated what became a very widespread habit in the next few years. It was a typical misfortune that Raleigh's supply boat that was sent out to Roanoke arrived only three days after all the settlers had already left with Sir Francis Drake.

In 1587 Raleigh sent another expedition to Virginia under John White, the artist, not to Roanoke but to Chesapeake Bay. This time women were sent out as members of the party. White, brilliant artist though he was (and his pictures are currently part of a brilliant exhibition in London), was totally lacking in leadership qualities. Unfortunately, and with typical misfortune, so far as Raleigh was concerned, the leading captain of the expedition, Juan Fernandez, mutinied and refused to take the settlers to Chesapeake Bay and insisted—contrary to his orders—on landing them all at Roanoke. The settlers then deposed White as leader and forced him to return to England, 112 of them remaining on Roanoke.

Raleigh's plans for stabilising the settlement were then completely scuppered by war with Spain and the advent of the Armada and it was not until 1590 that he could send another expedition, again under White, back to Roanoke to discover the fate of the 112 settlers. He arrived there in March 1590 to find the place completely deserted, a message having been carved into one of the trees indicating that the settlers had gone to another island, which was part of the Outer Banks. But the expedition gave up the search without finding any of them.

Raleigh then made a fatal mistake. He secretly married and had a child with one of Queen Elizabeth's ladies in waiting, Bess Throckmorton, without obtaining Elizabeth's consent. When in 1592 Elizabeth discovered what had happened, both Raleigh and Throckmorton were thrown into the Tower of London. They were, however, released on Sir Robert Cecil's advice about five weeks later. But it was then too late for Raleigh to re-enter the favours of Elizabeth, for she in the meantime had become much taken with Robert Devereux, Earl of Essex.

By this time Raleigh was very short of money and still in disgrace. In 1595, mindful that his monopoly of settlement and exploitation of Virginia would be lost unless he could establish continuity of settlement there, he mounted an expedition to Guiana in search of the fabled gold mine at El Dorado in order to replenish his finances and also for the purpose, on the way home, of receiving or rescuing the settlers who had been left at Roanoke in 1587. Misfortune stalked him yet again. He completely failed to find any gold in Guiana and bad weather prevented the vessel from getting to an anchorage in Virginia.

Two further rescue attempts were made to Roanoke in 1599 and 1602 but on the first occasion the vessel was prevented from getting past the Outer Banks by bad weather and on the second occasion no sign of the settlers could be found.

Then in March 1603 Queen Elizabeth died and, at the very same time, so did what remained of Raleigh's status. James I immediately dismissed him from his post as Captain of the Palace Guard. Within three months he was accused of plotting with one Lord Cobham to depose James I and replace him on the throne with Lady Arabella Stuart, who, it was intended, would make peace with Spain, which was of course a complete heresy, and permit Roman

Catholic toleration in England, which was also heresy. Raleigh was tried before Chief Justice Popham of the Common Pleas. He was convicted of treason, after the jury had been out for half an hour, on the strength of one unsigned statement by Cobham who confessed his own guilt as to that conspiracy and implicated Raleigh. In spite of Raleigh's complaints as to the insufficiency of the evidence and his request to cross-examine Cobham, this was refused. The prosecution was conducted by the Attorney-General, Sir Edward Coke, in a most intemperate manner. Raleigh was condemned to death in these words:

> You are to be conveyed to the place from whence you came and from thence to the place of execution, and there to be hanged till you are half dead, your members to be cut off, your bowels to be taken out and caste into the fire before your face (you being yet alive) your head to be cut off, your quarters to be divided into four parts, to be bestowed in four several places, and so (said my Lord Chief Justice) Lord have mercy upon your soul.

Shortly after I had been invited to come on this trip I found a 1648 edition of some notes taken at Raleigh's trial that contained verbatim passages from what passed, including the one that I have just quoted. It is clear that it was a completely unfair trial and I think you will appreciate this from the other passages that I am going to read out from it.

Of the opening by Sir Edward Coke, this was said:

> In Mr Attorney diverse things were observed which were said and used in his narration or evidence. Some captiously noted that he said this treason did tend not only to overthrow of true religion and destruction of all our souls but even to the loss of our goods, lands and lives: but it seemeth he meant reciprocally: others thought him full of impertinent phrases and compliments, and especially when he spoke of the King's issue or of the Lords after he said he would say nothing of them, then he would presently fall into gross and palpable adulation of them to their faces but in their commendations he spoke nothing but truth.

A little further on the note continues with regard to Coke's opening:

> All the assembly could have wished that he had not behaved himself so violently and bitterly nor used so great provocation to the prisoner which the better sort imputed to his zeal in the King's service and to the passion which overwhelmed him in the cause of his country as when he break forth into these and the like speeches: This horrible and detestable Traytor, this maine Traytor (for the rest were upon the bye), this instigator and seducer to treasons he that hath a Spanish heart, you are an odious man, see with what a whorish forehead he defends his faults. This is he that would take away the King and his cubs, oh abominable Traytor": but many prejudicate of Mr Attorney's nature would hardly be persuaded but those speeches proceeded out of the insolency of his own disposition given to triumph upon poor delinquents and men in misery. Honest men have reason to think the best and as the Attorney was noted so was the carriage of Raleigh most remarkable first to the Lords (principally to My Lord Cecil) humble yet not prostrate dutiful, yet not dejected for in some cases he would humbly thank them

for gracious speeches, in other acknowledged that their honours said true as in relating some circumstances:

Then it was further said of Raleigh:

But when it was insinuated that it was said that it would never be well until the King and his cubs were taken away he said that Mr Attorney used him basely, barbarously and rigorously and that he was a base slave and wretch that spoke the words, that he received comfort in these base words of Mr Attorney for he had hoped that it should be the worst that he should be able to do against him.

Later in the course of the trial the note records:

And my Lord Chief Justice said that one witness accusing himself too was very great testimony especially in this case for it was not to be imagined that my Lord Cobham would do himself so much harm as to adventure the loss of his honour, lands of so great worth and his life for any spleen to Sir Walter unless the matter were true and therefore the accusation was very strong against Sir Walter.

Still later Raleigh has reported to have said this:

But said he you tell me of one witness let me have him. Prove these practices by one witness and I will confess myself guilty to the King in a thousand treasons. I stand not upon the law, I defy the law if I have done these things I desire not to live: whether they be treasons by the law or no. Let me have my accuser brought to my face and if he will maintain it to my face I will confess my judgement.

Then the Lord Chief Justice, having been required to signify his opinion of the law on the evidence in this case, is reported to have said:

It was not the law to have the witness brought to his face, considering he accused himself also: to the which the rest of the judges agreed. Sir Walter replied: it was not against or contrary to the law: howsoever I do not expect it of duty and yet I say you should deal very severely with me if you should condemn me and not bring my accuser to my face.

And then a little later in the note it says this:

Why then my Lords let my accuser be brought and let me ask him a question and I have done: for it may be it will appear out of his own tale that his accusation cannot be true or he will be discovered by examination.... If my accuser were dead, or not within the land, it was something. But my accuser lives, and is in the house, and yet you will not bring him to my face.

In his final speech to the jury Raleigh said this:

If you would be content to be judged upon suspicions and inferences, if you would not have your accusation subscribed by your accuser. If you would not have your accuser brought to your face (being in the same house too) where you are arraigned. If you would be condemned by an accusation of one recanted and truly sorrowful for it, if you in my case would yield your bodies to torture, lose your lives, your wives and children and all your fortune upon so slender proof. Then I am ready to suffer all these things.

Although Raleigh had for many years become unpopular with the people because of his ostentation and conspicuous consumption, his conviction gave rise to enormous popular indignation, so great that James I was advised by Cecil to commute the death sentence. That left Raleigh in the Tower for 14 years, having been stripped of his Virginia monopoly and his lease of Durham House. During that time in December 1606 Captain Newport embarked upon yet another settlement expedition to Virginia. This one, astonishingly, was under the control of none other than Chief Justice Popham. The expedition arrived within the Outer Banks at the end of April 1607. A settlement in the name of James I was then declared at Jamestown. It is right to say that James I was totally disinterested in settlement in North America. Raleigh, however, had acted as unofficial consultant to the expedition, even from his quarters in the Tower. In his *Essay on Colonization* he wrote that settlers should educate the native people in law and religion and 'instruct them in the liberal arts of civility.'

Ten years later James I was so short of money that in 1617 he released Raleigh from the Tower in order for him to lead an expedition to the Orinoco River to try once again to take possession of the gold mine said to exist at Manoa. It was, however, a condition of that expedition that there was to be no invasion of Spanish territory, for James was then determined to negotiate a peace treaty with Spain. The expedition got to the Orinoco but Raleigh remained onboard and sent his second in command upstream with solders to find the gold mine. Completely contrary to orders, they carried out an attack on the Spanish garrison at San Thome. That was only partially successful and the expedition had to be abandoned at that point. Raleigh then returned to London and was at once thrown into the Tower. James I, to whom the Spanish ambassador had complained, immediately revoked the reprieve on Raleigh's death sentence. On 29 October Raleigh was executed at Westminster Old Palace.

Here is one final thought. According to an old diary of mine, on 21 June 1989 COMBAR was founded in principle at a meeting in the Devereux Public House which was built on what was originally the garden of Elizabeth's favourite, Robert Devereux, Earl of Essex and was only a few hundred yards from the site of Raleigh's Durham House on the Embankment.

I can only say that it is good to see that our transatlantic aspirations have so excellently succeeded where Raleigh's proved so hard to achieve.

6

Jamestown

MR JUSTICE DAVID STEEL

Delivered at the Renaissance Centre, Richmond on 13 April 2007

IT IS A great privilege for Charlotte and me to be your guests of honour at this unique meeting. It is also a pleasure to share that privilege with Tony and Angela Colman.

I think Tony and I can be justly proud of our child borne over 15 years ago. The initial features of COMBAR that I believe have resulted in its continuing success and buoyancy are twofold: first the decision that it should be properly financed so as to ensure a professional secretariat; second the decision that membership should be primarily by sets of chambers rather than individuals so as to ensure support across the whole spectrum of age and experience.

Any organisation with long-term aims must encourage the young, and I regard COMBAR's focus on this as having been conspicuously successful. Nonetheless, we now live in a world where a 21-year-old is almost treated as a child. How different things were 400 years ago.

Let us take John Smith who had been on board one of the three vessels that set out from London in December 1606, bound for Virginia with 140 hopeful colonists. We will see his statue tomorrow, gazing out over the James River at the site of Jamestown.

Smith had been born in 1580. He left home at 16. He immediately volunteered to fight for the Dutch seeking their independence from Spain. Thereafter, having spent about two years at sea, in 1600 he joined the Austrian army in order to fight against the Turks. He became an army captain at the age of 20.

Aged 22 he could be found fighting in Transylvania. However, he was wounded, captured and sold as a slave to a Turk. The Turk sent him to Istanbul as a gift to his girlfriend. The girlfriend fell in love with him but thereafter sent her brother to John Smith for army training. Captain Smith murdered the brother and escaped via Russia and Poland. He arrived back in England in 1604 at the ripe old age of 24. He was thus still in his twenties as the three vessels reached Virginia in 1606.

What remarkable courage was required to start a new life in the New World. The three ships had taken six weeks to get from England. Forty-five had died on the voyage leaving 100 men and four boys. During the voyage Smith had managed to get arrested for mutiny and was sentenced to hang. However, on landing, Smith's name emerged from secret orders as one of the designated councillors for the colony, thus leading to his reprieve.

What met the colonists ashore may have left those who had died en route feeling fortunate. Disease was rampant—typhus, malaria and dysentery. Food was in desperately short supply. Most of the water was unfit to drink. It was bitterly cold in winter and blisteringly hot in summer.

Needless to say Smith was soon in trouble and managed to get himself captured by the Indians in October 1607. Facing almost inevitable death he somehow succeeded in obtaining his reprieve by showing his magnetic compass to the Indian chief, Powatan.

It is ironic that the success of the colony was assured by two things that are regarded with such total disfavour today—tobacco and slavery. Again it is the youth of the participants which is so striking.

John Rolfe had survived a shipwreck off Bermuda in 1609. He was 24. He had come on to Virginia in a vessel built from the wreckage of the other vessels (a story immortalised by William Shakespeare in *The Tempest*) and found only 60 survivors at Jamestown.

Although Jamestown was nearly abandoned, by 1612 Rolfe had begun growing tobacco. He had obtained the seeds of *nicotiana tabacum* from South America. By 1614 the prospects of the colony were dramatically transformed by the first shipment of tobacco to arrive in London. In the meantime Rolfe had married Pocahontas, the daughter of Powatan, bringing a prolonged period of peace with the Indians.

By 1635 his son Thomas had reclaimed his father's tobacco plantations and the thousands of acres that were owned by his grandfather, Powatan. Tom Rolfe thus became the greatest landowner in Virginia. From the Rolfes are descended the great families of Virginia like the Randolphs, the Lewis, the Bollings and—wait for it—the Blairs.

By 1619 the cash crop of tobacco had led to a boom. So much so that 20 slaves were imported from Africa to help with the crops and 90 women from England to help with the population. The women were more expensive. They were 120lbs of tobacco each.

It is a fascinating tale. But I have said enough. I have very much in mind the advice of the mother whale to its offspring: 'Remember, it is while you are spouting that you are most likely to be harpooned.'

7

Speech delivered at University of Richmond School of Law on 11 April 2007[1]

RT HON LORD PHILLIPS OF WORTH MATRAVERS

ABOUT FOUR MONTHS ago I was dining with many who are here this evening in my Inn in London, the Middle Temple. It was 400 years to the day that there had set sail from London three tiny ships, bound for Virginia to found a colony pursuant to a Charter granted by King James on 10 April 1606. They made landfall at Chesapeake Bay on 26 April 1607. The expedition was not an unequivocal success. Those who embarked on it hoped to find gold. Instead they found disease, and most of them died. The expedition was attributable in large measure to the enthusiasm of one of my predecessors as Chief Justice, Sir John Popham, and had the support of other distinguished members of my Inn. I do not know how many lawyers there were among the very first settlers, nor how concerned they were with the rule of law. One of them a lawyer from the Middle Temple, George Percy, was to become a Governor of Virginia. Another member of my Inn, Sir Edwin Sandys was responsible for the Virginia Charter of 1606. This gave the first colonists 'all the liberties, franchises and immunities of English subjects' but no political rights. Much more significant was the subsequent 'Great Charter' of 1618, for which Sandys was also responsible. This entitled the settlers to institute a representative government under which they were assured freedom of speech, equality before the law and trial by jury'.

This, and the subsequent Charters of the American colonies, laid the ground for the Constitution of the United States. Lawyers, trained at the Inns of Court in London, for it became common for the leading families in the colonies to send their sons across the Atlantic for this purpose, contributed greatly to these Charters and indeed to the Constitution. Five members of my own Inn were signatories to the Declaration of Independence

[1] Speech previously published in the Autumn 2007 edition of the *University of Richmond Law Review*.

and no less than seven among those who signed the Constitution. It is that Constitution that embodies the rule of law in this country, and so we are celebrating this week the sowing of the seeds of the rule of law in the United States—seeds that were exported from my own country.

I first set foot on the Eastern seaboard in time of war—when I landed in New York as an evacuee in 1940. In times of war courts tend to be particularly diffident about questioning steps taken by the executive in the interests of national security. In the infamous case of *Liversedge v Anderson*[2] the House of Lords held that the Home Secretary could not be required to provide any justification for his exercise of the right to detain a man without trial because he believed that this was necessary because of his hostile associations.

The diffidence persisted in England even after the war.

In 1977 the Secretary of State served a deportation notice on a Mr *Hosenball* a US citizen working as a journalist on the ground that he had sought and obtained for publication information harmful to the security of the United Kingdom. When he refused to provide any details of this allegation Mr Hosenball sought judicial review of the decision. This was refused. This is what the great Lord Denning had to say:

> There is a conflict here between the interests of national security on the one hand and the freedom of the individual on the other. The balance between these two is not for a court of law. It is for the Home Secretary. He is the person entrusted by Parliament with the task. In some parts of the world national security has on occasions been used as an excuse for all sorts of infringements of individual liberty. But not in England. Both during the wars and after them, successive Ministers have discharged their duties to the complete satisfaction of the people at large.

Deference to the executive has not, I believe, been a notable feature of American jurisprudence. The difference between our two jurisdictions is, of course, that in this jurisdiction the rights of the individual are embodied in and protected by a written constitution. And you have a Supreme Court with jurisdiction to protect those rights to the extent of striking down legislation that is unconstitutional.

In my jurisdiction the constitution is largely unwritten. Parliament is supreme and the courts cannot refuse to give effect to legislation on the ground that it is unconstitutional.

Both our countries are now facing a new kind of conflict—that created by international terrorism. Yet despite the threat of terrorism, the UK courts are not showing the traditional deference to action taken by the executive in the interests of national security. The change in stance is largely attributable to the Human Rights Act 1998, which came into force in 2000. This Act was passed by the present administration soon after they came into office.

---

[2] [1942] 2 AC 206.

The Act allows individuals to invoke the provisions of the Human Rights Convention in disputes with government and requires judges to enforce Convention rights.

We cannot strike down legislation that conflicts with the Convention, but we can make a declaration that it is incompatible with the Convention. This is just about as good, because the government up to now has always responded to a declaration of incompatibility by changing the offending law. More significantly we now have to scrutinise executive action to ensure that it does not infringe human rights. We can no longer hold that actions taken in the interests of national security by the executive are not justiciable if those actions are alleged to infringe individual human rights.

The consequence of this has been a series of decisions of the courts holding unlawful legislation, statutory regulations and executive action designed to address the problem of terrorism.

The Human Rights Convention, as interpreted by the European Court at Strasbourg, poses a problem for the Government.

The Court has ruled in a case called *Chahal v United Kingdom*[3] that it is contrary to the Convention to deport an illegal immigrant if he will be at risk of torture or inhuman treatment if you send him home, however great a threat he may pose to your security. At the same time, it is contrary to the Convention to detain someone without trial simply because you have reasonable grounds to believe that he is involved in terrorism. The Convention permits a country to derogate from the latter obligation, but only 'to the extent strictly required by the exigencies of the situation ... in time of war or other public emergency threatening the life of the nation'.

After 9/11 the British Government decided that the threat of terrorism in Britain was such as to amount to a public emergency threatening the life of the nation and purported, on that ground, to derogate from the Convention.

It did so in respect of 'foreign nationals present in the United Kingdom who are suspected of being concerned in the commission, preparation or instigation of acts of international terrorism' or of being connected to terrorist groups and 'who are a threat to the security of the United Kingdom'. Relying on this derogation Parliament then passed an Anti-Terrorism Act in 2001 that permitted an alien to be detained indefinitely if the Home Secretary reasonably suspected that he was a terrorist and believed that he was a threat to national security, but was unable to deport him because he would be at risk of inhuman treatment in his own country.

The Home Secretary immediately certified that a number of aliens fell within the scope of the new Act, and they were locked up.

It was made plain to them that if they wanted to go back to their own countries they were free to go. They did not do so. What they did was to

---

[3] (1996) 23 EHRR 413.

exercise a right of appeal for which the Act made provision. The case is known simply by the initial of one of the appellants as 'A'.[4]

The procedure governing this appeal was unusual, involving a special judicial tribunal known as SIAC with special powers. Evidence, disclosure of which would have adverse implications for security, can be put before SIAC as 'closed' material.

This is not disclosed to the terrorist suspect. It is disclosed to a special advocate, whose duty it is to protect the suspect's interests, but once he has seen the material, the special advocate is no longer permitted to communicate with the suspect.

This procedure was challenged in a subsequent case, which came before a division of the Court of Appeal over which I presided. It was argued that it infringed the suspect's Convention right to a fair trial. We held that, in the particular circumstances, the procedure satisfied the test of fairness but this is a point on which the House of Lords has yet to rule.

Let me return to the case of A. The appeal of the alien terrorist suspects detained under the 2001 Act went right up to the House of Lords—our most senior court. They sat nine strong, instead of the usual five. The appeals were allowed. The majority of the Lords accepted that derogation from the Convention was possible in that there existed a 'public emergency threatening the life of the nation'. They held, however, that the terms of the derogation and of the Act were unlawful in that they went beyond what was 'strictly required by the exigencies of the situation. Three factors weighed particularly in their reasoning. The first was the importance that the United Kingdom has attached since at least Magna Carta to the liberty of the subject. The second was that the measures only applied to aliens.

There were plenty of terrorist suspects who were British subjects. How could it be necessary to lock up the foreign suspects without trial if it was not necessary to lock up the British suspects? Finally, the measures permitted those detained to opt to leave the country. If they were so dangerous, this did not seem logical, for they would be free to continue their terrorist activities overseas. And so the House of Lords quashed the derogation order and declared that the relevant provisions of the Act were incompatible with the Convention.

Lord Hoffmann alone did not consider that the terrorist threat amounted to 'a public emergency threatening the life of the nation'. In a Churchillian dissent he said:

> The real threat to the life of the nation, in the sense of a people living in accordance with its traditional laws and political values, comes not from terrorism but from laws such as these. That is the true measure of what terrorism may achieve.

[4] [2004] UKHL 56.

This statement was received with enthusiasm by the liberal groups but not by ministers, who considered that it violated the rule that a judge should not descend into politics.

Parliament's reaction to the Law Lords' decision was to pass a new Act; the Prevention of Terrorism Act 2005. This, among other things, empowers the Secretary of State to place restrictions on terrorist suspects by making them subject to control orders. The restrictions must not, however, be so severe as to amount to deprivation of liberty. A number of procedural safeguards are imposed by the Act, including automatic review of control orders by the court.

The first batch of control orders imposed by the Home Secretary required the suspects to stay confined within small apartments for 18 hours a day, and placed restrictions on where they could go and whom they could see in the remaining six hours. These orders were challenged and a Division of the Court of Appeal over which I presided upheld the finding of the judge of first instance that the orders were unlawful, in that the restrictions that they imposed amounted to deprivation of liberty.

The Home Secretary immediately imposed modified control orders in place of the old ones. These are not nearly as restrictive, and are specifically tailored to meet the situation of the particular suspect. There are currently 16 orders in force, of which seven relate to British subjects. On 15 occasions modifications have been made at the request of the suspect. On four occasions such a request has been refused.

The most significant difference between these and the previous control orders is that the curfew periods have been reduced to either 14, or in some cases 12, hours a day.

There have been a successful challenge to two of these new orders. The first was by a terrorist suspect known as E. He is one of the original detainees, and so has been subject to preventative measures for five years. In a very lengthy judgment Beatson J reached the conclusion that the cumulative effect of the restrictions imposed upon E amounted to deprivation of liberty, and so he quashed the order. The day before I left for the States the same judge quashed a second control order on the ground that it amounted to inhuman and degrading treatment. I have not yet seen that judgment and, in any event, I cannot comment on these cases, for they may well come before me in the Court of Appeal.

What I can do is to recount a comment of Charles Clarke, who was the Home Secretary at the time of some of the events that I have been describing, when giving evidence to a Parliamentary Committee. He said:

> The judiciary bears not the slightest responsibility for protecting the public and sometimes seems utterly unaware of the implications of their decisions for our society.

This added fuel to a picture that the media like to paint of the judges being at war with the executive.

It is a false picture. Our relations are in fact good, and I think that ministers understand—as perhaps the public does not—that judges are simply doing their best to apply the laws that Parliament has enacted, which include the law that requires them to give effect to the Human Rights Convention.

Debate about the justification for resorting to exceptional measures to deal with terrorism often focuses on the extreme case of the use of torture. What if a bomb has been placed that is likely to take countless lives and a terrorist has been caught who knows the location of the bomb? In such a situation cannot torture be justified in order to induce the terrorist to disclose where the bomb is hidden? The classic answer is that the law can never justify the use of torture, but in a situation such as that the executive might be forgiven for acting in a manner that was unlawful. A more difficult issue arose in the second round of litigation that had led to the Lords' famous decision in *A*. The issue was whether a court can receive evidence that has, or may have, been obtained by the use of torture. The Court of Appeal held that, in the circumstances of that case at least, it could, provided that the UK authorities were not party to the torture. On appeal to the House of Lords, sitting seven strong, the decision of the Court of Appeal was unanimously reversed. Their Lordships held that evidence obtained by torture was not admissible in an English court, whoever had done the torturing. There was, however, a critical issue on burden of proof. Should evidence be shut out whenever there is a risk that it may have been obtained by torture or only where the court is satisfied on balance of probabilities that is has been obtained by torture. By a slender majority of 4 to 3 the Lords decided that the latter was the position. This means that the English courts will admit evidence where there is a possibility, but not where there is a probability, that it has been obtained by torture.

At the end of last year, two gentlemen called Ahmad and Aswat were resisting extradition from the United Kingdom to the United States on the ground, inter alia, that they might find themselves subjected to 'extraordinary rendition', that is transfer to a foreign state in circumstances where there was a substantial risk that they would be subjected to torture. This submission required the English court to consider evidence as to the alleged practice of the United States, an area where in the past the court would have been reluctant to trespass.

The court considered quite a body of evidence and was not reassured by a statement from a federal prosecutor that

> the United States does not expel, return, or extradite individuals to countries where the United States believes that it is more likely than not that they will be tortured.

The court was, however, reassured by the fact that

> there was no evidence whatsoever that any person extradited to the United States from the United Kingdom or anywhere else, has been subsequently subjected to rendition, extraordinary of otherwise.

The court held that there was no reason why the two gentlemen should not be extradited.

This is not the only occasion on which the English court has had to take the unusual step of considering the legitimacy of what has been taking place on this side of the Atlantic.

Detainees at Guantanamo Bay included a number of British subjects. One of these, Mr Abbasi, instigated, with the aid of relatives, judicial review proceedings in the English court. He alleged that he was being unlawfully detained contrary to his fundamental human rights and sought a mandatory order that the Foreign Secretary should intervene on his behalf. The Foreign Secretary objected that the case was not justiciable, as it called for a review of his conduct of foreign affairs and this fell outside the jurisdiction of the court. He also contended that the English court would not investigate the legitimacy of the actions of a foreign sovereign state.

These submissions were upheld by the judge of first instance, who refused Mr Abbasi's application.

He appealed and I presided on that appeal. We allowed the appeal. We held that, where human rights were engaged, the English court could investigate the actions of a foreign sovereign state.

We heard the appeal at the time when the District Court of Columbia had ruled that the US courts had no jurisdiction over aliens detained at Guantanamo.

After reviewing both English and US authority, we commented[5]:

> [W]e do not find it possible to approach this claim for judicial review other than on the basis that, in apparent contravention of fundamental principles, recognised by both jurisdictions and by international law, Mr Abbasi is at present arbitrarily detained in a 'legal black hole' ... What appears to be objectionable is that Mr Abbasi should be subject to indefinite detention in territory over which the United States has exclusive control with no opportunity to challenge the legitimacy of his detention before any court or tribunal. It is important to record that the position may change when the appellate courts in the United States consider the matter.

And, of course, the position did change when, by a majority of six to three, the Supreme Court in *Rasul v Bush*[6] ruled that foreign nationals held at Guantanamo could use the US court system to challenge their detention.

I have described how in England the courts have repeatedly upheld challenges of actions taken by Parliament and the executive that are aimed at dealing with terrorist suspects.

There are parallels between what has been happening in my jurisdiction and what has been happening over here. The government can derogate from the Human Rights Convention if this is necessary to deal with a state

---

[5] [2002] EWCA Civ 1598 at para 64.
[6] (2004) 542 US 466.

of emergency threatening the life of the nation. After its first unsuccessful attempt to do so it has not tried again. The US Constitution prohibits Congress from suspending the 'Privilege of the Writ of Habeas Corpus' save where 'in Cases of Rebellion or Invasion public Safety may require it'. Congress has not suspended the writ of habeas corpus.

In *Hamdi v Rumsfeld*[7] Mr Hamdi, a US citizen, who had been declared an 'illegal enemy combatant', successfully invoked it. The Supreme Court held that he could not be held indefinitely in a US military prison without an opportunity to contest the allegations made against him by a neutral arbiter.

He had allegedly been captured fighting American forces in Afghanistan. Those forces were there pursuant to the resolution of Congress after 9/11 authorising the President to

> use all necessary and appropriate force against those nations, organizations or persons he determines planned, authorized, committed or aided the terrorist attacks or harboured such organizations or persons, in order to prevent any future acts of international terrorism against the United States.

Significantly in *Hamdi,* the Supreme Court recognised that this resolution empowered the detention of an enemy combatant in Afghanistan, even if he was a US citizen, pending the conclusion of hostilities there. It left unanswered the question of whether terrorist suspects who were not engaged in open warfare against the United States could lawfully be detained as 'enemy combatants'.

There are many who answer this description detained at Guantanamo; citizens of many different nations, many of them friendly to the United States, seized not only in Afghanistan, but in other countries where there are no current hostilities. Hundreds of detainees commenced applications for habeas corpus before or following the decision in *Rasul.* Congress responded by passing the Detainee Treatment Act which removed the jurisdiction of the courts to entertain applications for habeas corpus by aliens detained at Guantnamo.

It gave the Court of Appeals for the DC Circuit exclusive jurisdiction in respect of judicial review challenges by such detainees. In *Hamdan v Rumsfeld*[8] the Supreme Court held that this Act did not, on its true construction, apply to applications for habeas corpus made before the date that the Act came into effect—that is the vast body of applications that had already been made by detainees at Guantanamo. Hamdan, a Yemeni national, challenged the jurisdiction of the military commission before whom he was due to be tried for 'conspiracy to commit ... offences triable by military commission'.

---

[7] (2004) 542 US 507.
[8] (2006) 126 S Ct 2749.

The Supreme Court, by a majority, upheld this challenge, holding that there was no basis for ousting the jurisdiction of the Federal courts. It further found that the military commission, both in structure and in procedure, violated the provisions of both the Uniform Code of Military Justice and Article 3 of the Third Geneva Convention. Even if Hamdan were a dangerous individual who would cause great harm or death to innocent civilians given the opportunity, the executive was bound to comply with the prevailing rule of law in undertaking to try him and subject him to criminal punishment.

The reaction to this decision was the Military Commissions Act of 2006, signed into law by President Bush on 17 October 2006.

This sets up military commissions to try terror suspects found to be 'alien unlawful enemy combatants'. Section 7 of that statute amends s 2241 of title 28 of the United States Code to provide:

(1) No court, justice or judge shall have jurisdiction to hear or consider an application for a writ of habeas corpus filed by or on behalf of an alien detained by the United States who has been properly detained as an enemy combatant or is awaiting such determination.

(2) [Subject to certain exceptions] no court, justice or judge shall have jurisdiction to hear or consider any other action against the United States or its agents relating to any aspect of the detention, transfer, treatment, trial or conditions of confinement of an alien who is or was detained by the United States and has been determined by the United States to have been properly detained as an enemy combatant or is awaiting such determination.

Senator Cornyn commented of this section: 'It will finally get the lawyers out of Guantanamo Bay'.

On 20 February 2007 the US Court of Appeals for the DC Circuit handed down a decision in relation to claims for habeas corpus filed by detainees at Guantanamo before the Military Commissions Act came into force. The majority held that the Act removed the jurisdiction of the court to entertain their claims. One of the primary purposes of the Act had been to overrule *Hamdan* and it had done so.

The bone of contention between the majority, whose decision was given by Judge Randolph and Judge Rogers, who dissented, related to the effect of the Suspension Clause of the Constitution. The majority held that this clause protected the right to habeas corpus as it existed in 1789. At that date aliens held outside the jurisdiction of the United States had no such right to claim habeas corpus. In a lengthy dissent Judge Rogers expressed the view that the Act fell foul of the Suspension Clause. I must confess that I found his dissent somewhat more powerful than did the majority, who described it as 'full of holes'.

On 2 April, the Supreme Court, by a majority, denied petitions for certiorari by a number of Guantanamo detainees, who sought to challenge the constitutionality of the Military Commissions Act. But this was only on the procedural ground that the petitions were premature. The petitioners should first have sought relief from the Court of Appeals for the DC Circuit. We have not reached the end of the story.

What we have been seeing in each of our jurisdictions is a conflict between the desire of the executive to take certain pre-emptive measures against terrorist suspects and overriding legal principles—in our case the European Convention on Human Rights and in yours the Constitution of the United States.

In each case the courts have been called on to perform their duty of upholding the rule of law. Not everyone has appreciated this, giving that word each of its meanings.

The desirability of preventing terrorists from blowing up innocent citizens is one that we would all endorse. But terrorism is spawned by ideology. John Reid, our Home Secretary, in a recent speech said that we were living through what was 'at heart an ideological struggle'; a struggle between democracies and 'the core values of a free society' on the one hand and 'those who would want to create a society which would deny all the basic individual rights that we now take for granted' on the other.

At a lecture given at the London School of Economics last year, Shami Chakrabarti, the Director of the human rights group Liberty, observed:

> [T]he philosophy of post [Second World] war democrats is that of fundamental rights, freedoms and the rule of law. This is the legacy of Eleanor Roosevelt and ... of Winston Churchill ... If our values are truly fundamental and enduring, they have to be relevant whatever the level of the threat.

I share those sentiments, and would suggest that the legacy goes back further. It goes back to the day that the first settlers, whose arrival we are celebrating this week, landed in Chesapeake Bay.

Respect for human rights must, I suggest, be a key weapon in the ideological battle. Since the Second World War we in Britain have welcomed to the United Kingdom millions of immigrants, many of them refugees from countries whose human rights were not respected. The prosperity of the United States is built on immigrants who have been welcomed from every corner of the globe. It is essential that they, and their children and grandchildren, should be confident that their adopted countries treat them, and those who are nationals of the countries from which they have come, without discrimination and with due respect for their human rights. If they feel that they are not being fairly treated, their consequent resentment will inevitably result in the growth of those who, actively or passively, are prepared to support the terrorists who are bent on destroying the fabric of our society. The British Human Rights Act and the US Constitution are not merely their safeguards. They are foundations of our fight against terrorism.

Index